Latin Redux

OKLAHOMA SERIES IN CLASSICAL CULTURE

Oklahoma Series in Classical Culture

SERIES EDITOR
Ellen Greene, *University of Oklahoma*

ADVISORY BOARD
Ronnie Ancona, *Hunter College and CUNY Graduate Center*
Carolyn J. Dewald, *Bard College*
Thomas R. Martin, *College of the Holy Cross*
John F. Miller, *University of Virginia*
Richard F. Thomas, *Harvard University*
Charles B. Watson, *University of Oklahoma*

Redux

A Second-Year Grammar Review

BY SUSAN O. SHAPIRO

UNIVERSITY OF OKLAHOMA PRESS : NORMAN

Publication of this book is made possible in part through the generosity of Edith Kinney Gaylord.

Library of Congress Cataloging-in-Publication Data

Names: Shapiro, Susan O. (Susan Olfson), 1951– author.
Title: Latin redux : a second-year grammar review / by Susan O. Shapiro.
Description: First edition. | Norman : University of Oklahoma Press, 2024. Series: Oklahoma series in classical culture ; volume 65 | Includes bibliographical references. | Summary: "A review of the essentials of Latin grammar and syntax, focusing on the topics that second-year students typically struggle with or need help recalling. Includes lesson-reinforcing exercises, a Latin-to-English glossary, an English-to-Latin glossary, and a grammatical appendix"—Provided by publisher.
Identifiers: LCCN 2023054327 | ISBN 978-0-8061-9391-5 (paperback)
Subjects: LCSH: Latin language—Grammar—Textbooks. | Latin language—Syntax—Textbooks. | Latin language—Grammar—Problems, exercises, etc. | Latin language—Syntax—Problems, exercises, etc. | LCGFT: Textbooks. | Problems and exercises.
Classification: LCC PA2087.5 .S49 2024 | DDC 478.2—dc23/eng/20240325
LC record available at https://lccn.loc.gov/2023054327

Latin Redux: A Second-Year Grammar Review is Volume 65 in the Oklahoma Series in Classical Culture.

The paper in this book meets the guidelines for permanence and durability of the Committee on Production Guidelines for Book Longevity of the Council on Library Resources, Inc. ∞

Copyright © 2024 by the University of Oklahoma Press, Norman, Publishing Division of the University. Manufactured in the U.S.A.

All rights reserved. No part of this publication may be reproduced, stored in a retrieval system, or transmitted, in any form or by any means, electronic, mechanical, photocopying, recording, or otherwise—except as permitted under Section 107 or 108 of the United States Copyright Act—without the prior written permission of the University of Oklahoma Press. To request permission to reproduce selections from this book, write to Permissions, University of Oklahoma Press, 2800 Venture Drive, Norman OK 73069, or email rights.oupress@ou.edu.

To Phil Parisi,

my *sine qua non*

Contents

Acknowledgments	ix
Introduction	3
Chapter 1. Third Declension Nouns and Adjectives	4
Chapter 2. Deponent Verbs	16
Chapter 3. Participles	22
Chapter 4. Ablative Absolutes; Passive Periphrastic Conjugation	28
Chapter 5. Infinitives and Indirect Discourse	34
Chapter 6. Gerunds and Gerundives	40
Chapter 7. Subjunctive Forms	45
Chapter 8. Independent Uses of the Subjunctive	51
Chapter 9. Sequence of Tenses; Purpose and Result Clauses	56
Chapter 10. Indirect Commands; Fear Clauses	63
Chapter 11. Cum Clauses	69
Chapter 12. Conditions	74
Chapter 13. Relative Clauses	79
Chapter 14. Indirect Questions	87
Chapter 15. Subordinate Clauses in Indirect Discourse; Subjunctive of a Reported Reason	91
Grammatical Appendix	97
Latin-English Glossary	125
English-Latin Glossary	133
Chapter Index of "Lingua Latina Ubique" Entries	137

Acknowledgments

In the course of working on this Latin review grammar, I have benefited from the help of many people. I would first like to thank my friends and colleagues who have encouraged me along the way, especially those in the Utah Classical Association, who were eager to use the book in their own classes. I owe an enormous debt of gratitude to Alexis Christensen and Darryl Phillips, who read through the entire manuscript and gave me many valuable suggestions. I would also like to thank several generations of second-year Latin students at Utah State University, especially those from the Fall 2022 and Fall 2023 semesters, who worked through all of the lessons and eagerly pointed out problematic explanations and exercises that were particularly helpful. It goes without saying (and yet I do want to mention it) that all the remaining mistakes are my own. I am grateful to the editorial team at the University of Oklahoma Press, including Alessandra Jacobi Tamulevich, Steven B. Baker, and Marta Steele. Most of all, I owe special thanks to my husband, Philip Parisi, who encourages me in all my endeavors, and to whom this book is dedicated.

Latin Redux

Introduction

For most college-level Latin students, the third semester is their first opportunity to read a "real," unadulterated Latin text, usually Caesar or Cicero, although sometimes other authors are used. In most cases, these third-semester students have had to slog through an entire year of grammar and "made-up" Latin, and they are eager to finally read a real Latin author. For most students, this is the reason they chose to take Latin in the first place. But when they sit down to do their first translation in the fall, many find themselves unexpectedly frustrated and disheartened. Not only have they been away from Latin for three or four months (and so forgotten much of what they had learned), but many soon discover that their knowledge of Latin grammar and syntax, gained in most cases over the course of only two semesters, is not as comprehensive as they had previously thought. This review grammar is intended to help alleviate some of this frustration.

The fifteen chapters in this book focus on topics that students often do not learn thoroughly in the first year (such as gerunds and gerundives) as well as topics that are sometimes omitted in the first year through lack of time (such as subordinate clauses in indirect discourse). The lessons are presented in order of difficulty, but they can be used in any order, and each one can be used independently.

This book is meant to supplement readings in real Latin, which are usually the main focus of a third-semester class. It can be used with any Latin author. The book is intended to give students additional confidence in their ability to read Latin. Once the students have reviewed the topics in Latin grammar and syntax in this book, they will, I hope, be more confident (and even pleasantly surprised) when they find those same structures in their readings.

As a review text, this book is not comprehensive; rather, it focuses specifically on those aspects of Latin grammar that second-year students frequently find difficult. The goal is to lead intermediate Latin students through a targeted and intensive review that will enable them to read Latin with greater self-confidence and enjoyment.

I have added macrons (long marks) where appropriate to the vowels in the paradigms, both those in the chapters and in the Grammatical Appendix, since it is helpful for students to learn the long marks when they learn the forms. I have omitted the macrons elsewhere in the book, however, except where they are necessary for correct translation.

The "Lingua Latina Ubique" (Latin Language Everywhere) sections in each chapter are intended to be fun and to encourage students to become more aware of how much Latin we use every day.

1

Third Declension Nouns and Adjectives

Introduction

1. All Latin nouns and adjectives are grouped into categories (called declensions) according to the way they form their cases.

2. There are five declensions in Latin, determined by the characteristic vowel of their stem and by the ending of the genitive singular. The third declension is the most complex and usually gives students the most difficulty. Therefore, we devote this entire chapter to third declension nouns and adjectives.

Consonant-Stem Third Declension Nouns

3. One reason why students frequently have difficulties with the third declension is that there is a great variety in the nominative singular of these nouns, and the nominative singular frequently does not provide the base of the noun, which must be learned from the genitive singular. (The base must be learned because it is the form of the noun to which the case endings are added.)

4. The third declension is identified by its genitive singular form, which is the base + **is**.

5. Another difficulty with the third declension is that all three genders are represented in fairly equal numbers. There is no single characteristic gender for this declension.

6. Please learn the following four paradigms (or types) of third declension consonant-stem nouns:

Third Declension Nouns and Adjectives

	rēx, rēgis, m king	virtūs, virtūtis, f courage, virtue	homō, hominis, m man, human being	corpus, corporis, n body	case endings M&F	N
Sing						
nom/voc	rēx (rēg-s)	virtūs	homō	corpus	-s, —	—
gen	rēgis	virtūtis	hominis	corporis	-is	-is
dat	rēgī	virtūtī	hominī	corporī	-ī	-ī
acc	rēgem	virtūtem	hominem	corpus	-em	—
abl	rēge	virtūte	homine	corpore	-e	-e
Plu						
nom/voc	rēgēs	virtūtēs	hominēs	corpora	-ēs	-a
gen	rēgum	virtūtum	hominum	corporum	-um	-um
dat	rēgibus	virtūtibus	hominibus	corporibus	-ibus	-ibus
acc	rēgēs	virtūtēs	hominēs	corpora	-ēs	-a
abl	rēgibus	virtūtibus	hominibus	corporibus	-ibus	-ibus

7. Note that, while the nominative singular of the third declension can take many forms, the genitive singular is always the base + **-is**. Remove the **-is** ending from the genitive singular, and you have the base to which you may add the other case endings. (The neuter accusative singular is an exception; it looks just like the nominative singular.)

8. Many third declension nouns add an additional syllable to all forms that include the base, that is, all forms except the nominative singular (and the accusative singular of neuter nouns). See the above table for examples.

9. The nominatives and vocatives of all third declension nouns are always the same in both singular and plural. Also, the nominative and accusative plurals of all regular third declension nouns are always the same. The genitive plurals always end in **-um** (different from the **-orum** and **-arum** of the first and second declensions), and the dative and ablative plurals always end in **-ibus** (and they are always the same).

10. The gender of third declension nouns is frequently unpredictable, but nouns denoting human beings are usually masculine or feminine according to their meaning. Also note that abstract nouns ending in **-or** are usually masculine (e.g., **amor, amoris, m; labor, laboris, m**). (But note that the concrete noun **arbor, arboris** is feminine.) Also masculine are the nouns ending in **-tor**, which usually denote a doer (e.g., **victor, victoris, m; scriptor, scriptoris, m**).

11. Third declension nouns ending in **-tas, tatis; -tus, -tutis; -tudo, -tudinis; and -tio, -tionis** are all feminine. These are all abstract nouns. In fact, almost all abstract nouns in Latin are feminine (with the exception of the **amor, amoris** type, mentioned above).

12. There are several common neuter nouns that follow the **corpus, corporis** paradigm, including **tempus, temporis**, and **genus, generis**. Note that the nominatives of these nouns all have a short **u** (pronounced like the English word "us"), unlike the abstract feminine nouns of the **virtūs, virtūtis** type, which all have a long **u** (pronounced like the English word "loose").

I-stem Third Declension Nouns

13. Some third declension nouns are known as **i-stem** nouns, because they add a characteristic **i** in certain cases. Please learn the following paradigms:

	parisyllabics	parisyllabics	base in two consonants	neuters ending in -e, -al, or -ar	irregular
	cīvis, cīvis, m citizen	nūbes, nūbis, f cloud	urbs, urbis, f city	mare, maris, n sea	vīs, vīs, f force, strength
Sing					
nom/voc	cīvis	nūbēs	urbs	mare	vīs
gen	cīvis	nūbis	urbis	maris	vīs
dat	cīvī	nūbī	urbī	marī	vī
acc	cīvem	nūbem	urbem	mare	vim
abl	cīve	nūbe	urbe	marī	vī
Plu					
nom/voc	cīvēs	nūbēs	urbēs	maria	vīrēs
gen	cīv*ium*	nūb*ium*	urb*ium*	mar*ium*	vīr*ium*
dat	cīvibus	nūbibus	urbibus	maribus	vīribus
acc	cīves, -īs	nūbēs, -īs	urbēs, -īs	maria	vīrēs, -īs
abl	cīvibus	nūbibus	urbibus	maribus	vīribus

14. All **i-stem nouns** (that is, masculine, feminine, and neuter) add the **-i-** to the genitive plural, while **neuter i-stem** nouns also add an **-i-** to the nominative and accusative plural and ablative singular. Some authors (such as Vergil) frequently use an alternative **-is** ending for the accusative plural of masculine and feminine nouns.

15. As you can see from the table, most i-stem third declension nouns belong to one of three main types:

    (a) *Parisyllabics*: These masculine and feminine i-stem nouns have the **same number of syllables** in their nominative and genitive singular forms (unlike most third declension nouns). These will usually have **-is, -is** for the nominative and genitive (such as **civis, civis, m** - citizen; or **ignis, ignis, m** - fire) or **-es, -is**, (such as **nubes, -is, f** - cloud; or **vulpes, -is, f** - fox).

Third Declension Nouns and Adjectives

 (b) *Base ending in two consonants:* Masculine and feminine nouns whose nominative singular ends in **-s** or **-x** and whose base ends in two consonants (such as **ars, artis, f** - art; **pars, partis, f** - part; or **dens, dentis, m** - tooth).

 (c) *Neuter nouns with a nominative singular ending in -e, -al, or -ar.* Examples include **animal, animalis, n** - animal; **calcar, calcaris, n** - spur.

16. There are also a few irregular i-stem nouns, such as **vis, vis, f** - strength. Please note that **vis, vis** is a parisyllabic, feminine, third declension, i-stem noun, and that it is an abstract noun (denoting something intangible). The accusative singular is the origin of the English noun "vim" (as in the phrase "vim and vigor"). Do not confuse this feminine, third declension i-stem with the masculine, second declension noun, **vir, viri, m** - man. The two nouns are compared in the table below.

	vir, virī, m - man	**vīs, vīs, f** - strength
Sing		
nom/voc	vir	vīs
gen	virī	vīs
dat	virō	vī
acc	virum	vim
abl	virō	vī
Plu		
nom/voc	virī	vīres
gen	virōrum	vīrium
dat	virīs	vīribus
acc	virōs	vīrēs
abl	virīs	vīribus

As you can see, although some of the forms of these two words are similar, **none of the forms is exactly the same**.

Third Declension Adjectives

17. All adjectives in Latin are either of the combined first and second declension type or the third declension. There are no fourth or fifth declension adjectives.

18. Remember that Latin adjectives modify nouns according to gender, number, and case, *not* spelling (as in the modern Romance languages). So a good man would be **bonus vir** (or **bonus homo**) and a strong woman would be **fortis femina**. In each of these examples, the adjective agrees with its noun in gender, number, and case, but not in spelling.

19. Please learn the following paradigms for Third Declension Adjectives:

	two endings fortis, forte - strong		three endings ācer, ācris, ācre - sharp		one ending potēns - powerful		comparatives fortior, fortius - stronger	
	M&F	N	M&F	N	M&F	N	M&F	N
Sing								
nom	fortis	forte	ācer, ācris	ācre	potēns		fortior	fortius
gen	fortis		ācris		potentis		fortiōris	
dat	fortī		ācrī		potentī		fortiōrī	
acc	fortem	forte	ācrem	ācre	potentem	potēns	fortiōrem	fortius
abl	fortī		ācrī		potentī		fortiōre	
Plu								
nom	fortēs	fortia	ācrēs	ācria	potentēs	potentia	fortiōrēs	fortiōra
gen	fortium		ācrium		potentium		fortiōrum	
dat	fortibus		ācribus		potentibus		fortiōribus	
acc	fortēs, -īs	fortia	ācrēs, -īs	ācria	potentēs, -īs	potentia	fortiōrēs	fortiōra
abl	fortibus		ācribus		potentibus		fortiōribus	

20. Note that all third declension adjectives are **i-stems**; they end in **-i** (rather than **-e**) in the ablative singular, and they have an extra **i** in the genitive plural. Neuter nominative and accusative plurals also end in **-ia**. Also, the M&F accusative plurals have an alternative **-is** ending, just as **i-stem** nouns do.

21. Most third declension adjectives are two-ending adjectives like **fortis, forte**. That is, they have one set of endings for masculine and feminine nouns, and another set for neuter nouns. Note that the genitive, dative, and ablative singulars and the genitive, dative, and ablative plurals are the same for both M&F and N. The vocatives are the same as the nominatives.

22. Some third declension adjectives have three endings in the nominative singular (like **acer, acris, acre**) and some have only one ending in the nominative (like **potens**). But these variations occur only in the nominative singular. In all other cases these adjectives are formed exactly like **fortis, forte**.

23. Comparative adjectives are formed by adding **-ior** to the base (M&F) or **-ius** to the base (N). Note that the third declension **comparative** adjectives are **NOT i-stems**.

24. Present participles (to be discussed in Chapter 3) have the same form as the adjective **potens,** but they have an **-e** instead of an **-i** in the ablative singular when used as participles.

25. Note that the superlative forms of the adjectives, since they are first and second declension adjectives, are not reviewed here.

Lingua Latina Ubique

Carpe diem - Seize the day! This aphorism is from Horace's *Odes* 1.11.8. In this poem, Horace urges us not to worry too much about the future, but to make the most of the present moment.

This line was famously quoted in the 1989 film *Dead Poets Society*, by the English teacher John Keating, played by Robin Williams.

E pluribus unum - Out of many, one. This is the official motto of the United States of America, and it refers to the idea that the original thirteen colonies came together to form a single nation.

Magnum opus - The great work or **masterpiece.** This term can refer to any great work in literature, music, or art, but it is often used to describe the most famous work by an artist or writer, for which he or she is most well known

Note that the second declension adjective agrees with the third declension noun grammatically, but they do not have the same ending because they belong to different declensions.

Magna cum laude - With great praise. Many American universities give honors to their top bachelor's degree candidates using a Latin system:
    cum laude - with praise
    magna cum laude - with great praise
    summa cum laude - with the highest praise

Note that in **magna cum laude** and **summa cum laude**, the second declension adjectives modify a third declension noun, all in the ablative case. In Latin, when a preposition (such as **cum**) governs both an adjective and a noun, the adjective is often placed before the preposition.

Chapter I

Exercises

A. Write the correct Latin forms in the table below.

	nom sing	gen sing	abl sing	nom plu	gen plu
1	bonus vir				
2	fortis puella				
3	ferox canis				
4	potens rex				
5	magnum opus				
6	fortior animal				
7	gravis civis				
8	magna vis				
9	iustus homo				
10	candida urbs				

Third Declension Nouns and Adjectives

B. Write the correct Latin forms in the table below.

	English	nom sing	gen sing	acc sing	gen plu	abl plu
1	pretty cat					
2	white cloud					
3	shining star					
4	tragic poem					
5	brave girl					
6	wild sea					
7	just treaty					
8	strong soldier					
9	sharper mind					
10	dark night					
11	easier work					
12	larger book					

Chapter I

C. In the sentences below, fill in the blanks with the correct forms of the Latin words you are given. Then translate the sentence. (Be ready to identify the correct gender, number, and case of the Latin words you have used to fill in the blanks.)

1. Aeneas erat _____ _____ [fortis vir] qui habitabat in Troia, _____ _____ [candida urbs].

   _____

   _____

2. Troia erat _____ et _____ _____ [bella et magna urbs] in Asia, in qua _____ _____ [multus Troianus] habitabant.

   _____

   _____

3. Graeci navigaverunt ad Troiam et _____ _____ _____ [illa magna urbs] decem annos obsiderunt.

   _____

   _____

4. Quando Graeci ceperant _____ _____ [opulenta Troia], Aeneas ex urbe effugit cum _____ _____ [paucus socius].

   _____

   _____

Third Declension Nouns and Adjectives

5. _____ _____ [paucus socius] navigaverunt ad Italiam et condiderunt _____ _____ [nova urbs], quam appellaverunt Lavinium, ab nomine _____ [dulcis] uxoris Aeneae, Lavinia.

_____

_____

_____

6. _____ [fortis] Troiani, qui habitabant in _____ _____ [nova urbs], Lavinio, nunc appellati sunt Latini, ab nomine _____ [prudens] Latini, patris Laviniae.

_____

_____

_____

7. Eo tempore, Etrusci erant _____ _____ [fortis populus] in Italia. Illi metuebant _____ _____ [nova urbs], Lavinium, quod Latini erant _____ _____ [fortis populus]. Latini crescebant _____ et _____ [fortior et potentior] in dies (every day).

_____

_____

_____

_____

CHAPTER I

8. Etrusci et Latini pugnaverunt in _____ et _____ _____ [multa et ferox pugna]. Etrusci victi sunt; victores tamen _____ _____ [fortis dux] Aenean amiserunt.

_____

_____

_____

_____

9. Aeneas casus est in _____ _____ [ferox pugna], sed post _____ _____ [ea pugna], Latini et socii non potuerunt videre Aenean.

_____

_____

10. Illius causā, multi dicebant _____ _____ [pius Aeneas] ad deos transisse.

_____

_____

(Note that this sentence uses indirect statement.)

Third Declension Nouns and Adjectives

11. Lavinia inde regnavit inter Latinos _____ _____ [multus annus]. Tandem Ascanius, filius Aeneae et Laviniae, condidit _____ _____ [nova urbs] quae Alba Longa appellata est.

_____

_____

_____

D. Translate the following English sentences into Latin.

1. The stories about ancient Romans are interesting, but the story about the fierce wolves is more frightening.

2. Some books about Roman history are too long.

3. The Romans fought many battles and conquered many men.

4. The proud king ignored the bad omens and invaded the neighboring country.

5. The aqueducts brought water from the distant mountains into the crowded cities.

2

Deponent Verbs

1. **Deponent verbs** are unusual because they have passive forms but active meanings. The name "deponent" comes from the Latin verb **depono** - to put aside, because they have "put aside" their passive meaning and taken up an active one. They may have originally been reflexive verbs.

2. The forms of deponent verbs are exactly like the passive forms of the regular conjugations, but because the passive forms are used less frequently, it will be helpful to review them here. Note that the second person singular forms of the present, imperfect, and future tenses have an alternative **-re** spelling, just as the passive forms of regular conjugations do.

3. **Deponent verbs have only three principal parts**: first person singular of the present tense, the present infinitive, and the first person singular of the perfect indicative.

4. Deponent verbs form their present infinitive exactly like the present passive infinitive of the regular conjugation. For the first, second, and fourth conjugations, there is a **long -i** in place of the **final -e**. For the third conjugation, the long **-i** stands in place of the final **-ere**.

5. Please learn the following paradigms.

Principal Parts of Deponents

conj	pres indic	pres infin	perf indic
1st	cōnor, I try	cōnarī, to try	cōnātus sum, I tried
2nd	polliceor, I promise	pollicērī, to promise	pollicitus sum, I promised
3rd	sequor, I follow	sequī, to follow	secūtus sum, I followed
3rd -io	prōgredior, I move forward	prōgredī, to move forward	prōgressus sum, I moved forward
4th	partior, I share	partīrī, to share	partītus sum, I shared

Deponent Verbs

6. In the perfect indicative, the **participle** and the form of **sum** must agree with the subject. So **Cornelia conata est** (Cornelia tried) and **Milites conati sunt** (the soldiers tried).

7. Please learn the following paradigms:

Present Tense

Sing	1st conj	2nd conj	3rd conj	3rd -io conj	4th conj
1st	cōnor	polliceor	sequor	prōgredior	partior
2nd	cōnāris (-re)	pollicēris (-re)	sequeris (-re)	prōgredieris (-re)	partīris (-re)
3rd	cōnātur	pollicētur	sequitur	prōgreditur	partītur
Plu					
1st	cōnāmur	pollicēmur	sequimur	prōgredimur	partīmur
2nd	cōnāminī	pollicēminī	sequiminī	prōgrediminī	partīminī
3rd	cōnantur	pollicentur	sequuntur	prōgrediuntur	partiuntur

Imperfect Tense

Sing	1st conj	2nd conj	3rd conj	3rd -io conj	4th conj
1st	cōnābar	pollicēbar	sequēbar	prōgrediēbar	partiēbar
2nd	cōnābāris (-re)	pollicēbāris (-re)	sequēbāris (-re)	prōgrediēbāris (-re)	partiēbāris (-re)
3rd	cōnābātur	pollicēbātur	sequēbātur	prōgrediēbātur	partiēbātur
Plu					
1st	cōnābāmur	pollicēbāmur	sequēbāmur	prōgrediēbāmur	partiēbāmur
2nd	cōnābāminī	pollicēbāminī	sequēbāminī	prōgrediēbāminī	partiēbāminī
3rd	cōnābantur	pollicēbantur	sequēbantur	prōgrediēbantur	partiēbantur

Future Tense

Sing	1st conj	2nd conj	3rd conj	3rd -io conj	4th conj
1st	cōnābor	pollicēbor	sequar	prōgrediar	partiar
2nd	cōnāberis (-re)	pollicēberis (-re)	sequēris (-re)	prōgrediēris (-re)	partiēris (-re)
3rd	cōnābitur	pollicēbitur	sequētur	prōgrediētur	partiētur
Plu					
1st	cōnābimur	pollicēbimur	sequēmur	prōgrediēmur	partiēmur
2nd	cōnābiminī	pollicēbiminī	sequēminī	prōgrediēminī	partiēminī
3rd	cōnābuntur	pollicēbuntur	sequentur	prōgredientur	partientur

Perfect Tense

Sing	1st conj	2nd conj	3rd conj	3rd -io conj	4th conj
1st	cōnātus sum	pollicitus sum	secūtus sum	prōgressus sum	partītus sum
2nd	cōnātus es	pollicitus es	secūtus es	prōgressus es	partītus es
3rd	cōnātus est	pollicitus est	secūtus est	prōgressus est	partītus est
Plu					
1st	cōnātī sumus	pollicitī sumus	secūtī sumus	prōgressī sumus	partītī sumus
2nd	cōnātī estis	pollicitī estis	secūtī estis	prōgressī estis	partītī estis
3rd	cōnātī sunt	pollicitī sunt	secūtī sunt	prōgressī sunt	partītī sunt

Pluperfect Tense

Sing	1st conj	2nd conj	3rd conj	3rd -io conj	4th conj
1st	cōnātus eram	pollicitus eram	secūtus eram	prōgressus eram	partītus eram
2nd	cōnātus erās	pollicitus erās	secūtus erās	prōgressus erās	partītus erās
3rd	cōnātus erat	pollicitus erat	secūtus erat	prōgressus erat	partītus erat
Plu					
1st	cōnātī erāmus	pollicitī erāmus	secūtī erāmus	prōgressī erāmus	partītī erāmus
2nd	cōnātī erātis	pollicitī erātis	secūtī erātis	prōgressī erātis	partītī erātis
3rd	cōnātī erant	pollicitī erant	secūtī erant	prōgressī erant	partītī erant

Future Perfect Tense

Sing	1st conj	2nd conj	3rd conj	3rd -io conj	4th conj
1st	cōnātus erō	pollicitus erō	secūtus erō	captus erō	partītus erō
2nd	cōnātus eris	pollicitus eris	secūtus eris	captus eris	partītus eris
3rd	cōnātus erit	pollicitus erit	secūtus erit	captus erit	parītus erit
Plu					
1st	cōnātī erimus	pollicitī erimus	secūtī erimus	captī erimus	partītī erimus
2nd	cōnātī eritis	pollicitī eritis	secūtī eritis	captī eritis	partītī eritis
3rd	cōnātī erunt	pollicitī erunt	secūtī erunt	captī erunt	partītī erunt

8. **Peculiarities of participles of deponents:** Participles and gerundives will be formally introduced in Chapters 3 and 6, but please note the following about the participles of deponents:

Most deponent forms have passive forms with active meanings, but present active and future active participles of deponents have active forms with active meanings.

Gerundives (i.e., future passive participles) of deponent verbs have passive forms with passive meanings.

Lingua Latina Ubique

Non sequitur - It does not follow. This expression was originally used to denote a logical fallacy, when a conclusion does not follow from the premises. But today we use it to refer to any statement or comment that is not related to the topic at hand. Sometimes people use a **non sequitur** on purpose to change the topic of conversation or to inject a note of humor in a serious conversation; other times people may use a non sequitur unwittingly.

Here is an example: "You're right that Latin takes time to learn, but did you know I have a cat?"

Note that **sequitur** is from the deponent verb **sequor**.

Sine qua non - Without which not. This phrase is used to describe something that is essential to the existence of something else. For example, "If you want to bake a cake, flour is the **sine qua non**." In other words, flour is the essential ingredient, without which there would be no cake.

Note that the preposition **sine** takes the ablative, so **qua** in this phrase is the ablative singular of the feminine version of the relative pronoun (**qui, quae, quod**). The feminine **qua** is used to refer to the implied noun **causa** (cause or reason).

Quorum. The minimum number of members of a group that must be present to conduct the business of that group. For example, a **quorum** could refer to the minimum number of voters who must cast votes if an election is to be valid.

The Latin word is the genitive plural of the relative pronoun **qui** (who), so the word literally translates as "of whom."

Placebo - I shall please. This noun (in English) is the first person singular, future active indicative form of the Latin verb, **placeo, placere** - to please. In medicine, a placebo is a treatment or substance that has no therapeutic value (such as a sugar pill) that is given to patients who believe that it will help them. The **placebo** effect, in which patients who have received a **placebo** actually feel better, has been well documented in medical studies.

Placebos are often given to the control group in medical trials, so patients will not know whether or not they are receiving the active substance. The use of **placebos** can raise ethical questions, so it is important that participants in the trial are aware that they might be receiving a **placebo**.

Nocebo - I shall harm. A related term, **nocebo** is the first person singular, future active indicative of the Latin verb, **noceo, nocere** - to harm. As you might guess, a **nocebo** is a treatment or substance that the patient expects to cause harm, but it is actually an inert substance. Just as with a **placebo**, a **nocebo** can cause a patient to feel worse after taking it, but this is due to the patient's own expectation of harm, rather than to the **nocebo** itself.

Chapter 2

Exercises

A. Write the correct Latin forms in the table below. The first row is done for you.

	conj	verb	pers	pres	fut	imperf	perf	pluperf
1.	1st	conor	3rd sing	conatur	conabitur	conabatur	conatus est	conatus erat
2.	3rd	sequor	1st plu					
3.	2nd	fateor	2nd sing					
4.	3rd -io	patior	3rd plu					
5.	4th	experior	1st sing					
6.	2nd	vereor	2nd plu					
7.	1st	miror	1st plu					
8.	3rd	proficiscor	1st sing					
9.	3rd -io	progredior	2nd sing					
10.	4th	partior	1st plu					

B. Translate the following Latin sentences into English.

1. Venus auxilium ad filium, Aenean, pollicetur.

2. Ille rex urbem defendere non conatus est.

3. Multi populi magnum opus Vergilii mirantur.

4. Hunc cibum partiemur quem amici nostri nobis dederunt.

5. Nisi eis auxilium celeriter feres, morientur.

Deponent Verbs

6. Incolae eius regionis ferocem leonem magnopere verebantur.

7. Hercules ferox ferocem leonem non veritus est.

8. Omnes laeti erant quando leo necatus est ab Hercule.

9. Magnum pretium quod populi polliciti erant Herculi dederunt.

10. Parvus puer patrem diutius non sequebatur.

C. Translate the following English sentences into Latin.

1. The commander followed the enemy, who had fled from the camp.

2. Many people wondered at the courage of Hercules.

3. The commanders will not advance far from the camp.

4. Will the soldiers wander for a long time through the forest?

5. Apollo promised immortality to Hercules.

3

Participles

1. **Most verbs have four participles:** the present active, the perfect passive, the future active, and the future passive.

2. It is important to **know the proper stem for each participle, as well as the proper ending.** The present active and future passive are built on the present stem, while the perfect passive and future active are built on the participial stem, as can be seen from the following table.

	active	passive
pres	present stem + **-ns, -ntis**	———
perf	———	participial stem + **-us, -a, -um**
fut	participial stem + **-urus, -ura, -urum**	present stem + **-ndus, -nda, -ndum**

3. The **present stem** is the **second principal part** (present active infinitive) without the **-re**. The participial stem is the **fourth principal part** without the **-us, -a, -um**. In fact, in most cases, the fourth principal part is the neuter form of the perfect passive participle.

4. The differences in the stems can best be seen through the participles of **ago, agere, egi, actum:**

	active	passive
pres	**agēns, agentis**, doing	———
perf	———	**āctus, -a, -um**, having been done
fut	**āctūrus, -a, -um**, about to do	**agendus, -nda, -ndum**, ought to be done, should be done

5. Note that in the third **-io and fourth conjugations,** the ending of the present participle is actually -**ens** (not simply -**ns**).

PARTICIPLES

6. Please learn the following paradigms.

	active	passive
pres	**amāns, amantis**, loving	———
	monēns, monentis, warning	———
	dūcēns, ducentis, leading	———
	capiēns, capientis, taking	———
	audiēns, audientis, hearing	———
perf	———	**amātus, -a, -um**, having been loved
	———	**monitus, -a, -um**, having been warned
	———	**ductus, -a, -um**, having been led
	———	**captus, -a, -um**, having been taken
	———	**audītus, -a, -um**, having been heard
fut	**amātūrus, -a, -um**, about to love	**amandus, -a, -um**, should be loved
	monitūrus, -a, -um, about to warn	**monendus, -a, -um**, should be warned
	ductūrus, -a, -um, about to lead	**dūcendus, -a, -um**, should be led
	captūrus, -a, -um, about to take	**capiendus, -a, -um**, should be taken
	audītūrus, -a, -um, about to hear	**audiendus, -a, -um**, should be heard

7. **Declension of participles:** The present participle is declined like a one-ending third declension adjective (e.g., **potens**) except that it has an **-e** in the ablative singular, instead of an **-i**. All other participles are first and second declension.

8. **Participles are verbal adjectives**, i.e., they are adjectives formed on the base of a verb. As adjectives, participles agree in gender, number, and case with the noun they modify, and they can be used in place of a noun (e.g., **sapiens** - a wise man, **ducens** - a leader). But because they are formed on the base of a verb, they have tense and voice and they can take a direct object.

9. The **future active participle** is translated as "about to verb." The form of the future active participle is easy to remember if you note that the English word "future" is from **futurus, -a, -um** (the future active participle of **sum**).

10. The **future passive participle** can be translated as "should be verbed," "ought to be verbed," "must be verbed," or something similar. **The future passive participle always has the sense of obligation or necessity.** This can be seen in English derivatives, such as *agenda* (things to be done) or *memoranda* (things to be remembered).

11. When a participle introduces a subordinate clause, the **tense of a participle is relative to the tense of the main verb**.

    A present participle shows action **at the same time** as the main verb.
    A perfect participle shows action **prior to** the main verb.
    A future participle shows action that will occur **after** the main verb.

    Examples:
    Dido, videns Aenean, eum miratur.   Dido, seeing Aeneas, admires him.
    Dido, videns Aenean, eum mirata est. Dido, seeing Aeneas, admired him.

    In both of the above examples, the present participle (**videns**) shows action occurring at the same time as the main verb, no matter whether the main verb is in the present or perfect tense.

    Aeneas, visus a Didone, laetatur.   Aeneas, having been seen by Dido, is happy.
    Aeneas, visus a Didone, laetatus est. Aeneas, having been seen by Dido, was happy.

    In both of the above examples, the perfect passive participle (**visus**) shows action that takes place before the main verb, no matter whether the main verb is in the present or perfect tense.

12. Strictly speaking, Latin participles introduce phrases, not clauses (since a clause must have both a noun and a verb). But, since Latin participles are formed from verbs, and most Latin participial phrases are translated into subordinate clauses in English, we will say (speaking loosely) that Latin participles can introduce subordinate clauses.

13. Remember that deponent verbs have present and future **active participles** with **active meanings**: **conans** - trying, **conaturus** - about to try.

Lingua Latina Ubique

Vox populi - Voice of the people. This Latin phrase refers to the opinion of most ordinary people. In journalism, the phrase is sometimes shortened to **vox pop** and refers to an interview with the "man on the street."

The implication is that the views of ordinary people show a kind of wisdom that sometimes evades the experts. This view is expressed in the proverb **Vox populi, vox Dei** (The voice of the people is the voice of God). Do you agree?

Casus belli - Cause of war or **occasion for war.** This Latin phrase describes either an act or event that provokes a war or a reason given to justify a war.

The term came into use in the sixteenth and seventeenth centuries as part of the "just war" theory, i.e., the attempt to define the reasons that can justify a nation's going to war.

Excelsior. This word (which is the masculine and feminine singular comparative adjective of **excelsus** - high) literally means **higher**, but it is colloquially translated as **ever higher** or **onward and upward**. It refers to the idea of constantly striving for higher goals through hard work and persistence.

This word is the motto of New York State, and it is also the title of an 1841 poem by Henry Wadsworth Longfellow, who was supposedly inspired by New York's motto. Here is the first stanza of the Longfellow poem:

> The shades of night were falling fast,
> As through an Alpine village passed
> A youth, who bore, 'mid snow and ice,
> A banner with the strange device,
> Excelsior!

Chapter 3

Exercises

A. In the table below, write the present active, perfect passive, future active, and future passive participles of each verb in the nominative, masculine singular.

	pres active	perf passive	fut active	fut passive
1. moneo				
2. verto				
3. munio				
4. duco				
5. do				
6. capio				
7. pono				
8. audio				
9. premo				
10. gero				
11. scio				
12. facio				
13. video				
14. finio				
15. laudo				

B. Translate the following participial phrases.

1. poetae scribentes – _____

2. matres locutas – _____

3. saxa iacta – _____

4. puellis ducentibus – _____

PARTICIPLES

5. homo lecturus libros – _____

6. senes dicturos sententiam – _____

7. pater baculum tenens – _____

8. liberorum in lectis dormientium – _____

9. canibus latraturis ad leonem – _____

10. nomen appellandum – _____

C. Translate the following sentences. Identify each participle and its type.

1. Senator voces populorum Caesarem laudantes audivit.

2. Graecia capta ferum victorem cepit. (Horace, *Epistles* 2.1.156)

3. Puer per agros ambulans serpentem vidit.

4. Haec urbs nobis non placet, et mox ad alium locum cum amicis profecturi sumus.

5. Res publica cibum militibus in castris mansuris dedit.

6. Epistulam de his rebus mox missurus sum.

7. Epistula de his rebus mittenda erit vobis.

8. Liberi ad ludum a paedagogo ducti multa discent.

9. Mater missura epistulam e domo ambulabat.

10. Consules laudem viro veritatem locuto dederunt.

D. Translate the following English sentences into Latin.

1. We saw the ship sailing to the land.

2. We hear the voices of the citizens demanding food.

3. Everyone saw the lion having been killed.

4. The sailors, about to sail on the sea, prepared their ships.

5. The soldiers, desiring to cross the river, built a bridge.

4

Ablative Absolutes; Passive Periphrastic Conjugation

1. In the last chapter we learned about participles. Two important uses of the participle in Latin are the **ablative absolute** and the **passive periphrastic conjugation**.

Ablative Absolutes

2. An ablative absolute has at least two words: a noun (or pronoun) in the ablative case and a participle agreeing with it. The ablative absolute forms a subordinate clause that **explains the circumstances under which the action of the main clause takes place.**

3. The ablative absolute is **grammatically separate from the rest of the sentence** (that is why it is called "absolute"). In other words, **the ablative absolute does not agree grammatically with any other word in the sentence.**

4. An ablative absolute can contain any type of participle (present active, perfect passive, future active, or future passive), but **the vast majority use the perfect passive participle**.

5. **Ablative absolutes with the perfect passive participle** can be translated using the following formula: **"with the noun having been participled."** Here are some examples.

Duce capto, milites fugerunt.	With the leader having been captured, the soldiers fled.
His rebus auditis, populus celebravit.	With these things having been heard, the people celebrated.
Populo metu oppresso, Hercules leonem necavit.	With the people having been oppressed by fear, Hercules killed the lion.

6. As you can see from these examples, the ablative absolute explains the circumstances under which the action of the main clause takes place, but it is not grammatically

connected to the main clause. The third example also shows that an ablative absolute can have more than two words.

7. Although most ablative absolutes contain a perfect passive participle, **any type of participle can be used**. The formula for translation will change accordingly. Consider the following examples.

Magistro docente, discipuli discebant.	With the teacher teaching, the students were learning.
Milite morituro, puella lacrimat.	With the soldier about to die, the girl weeps.
Cicerone consule, res publica servata est.	With Cicero being consul, the republic was saved.

8. The last example illustrates a type of ablative absolute in which the participle, "being," is understood. (The Latin verb **sum** has only one participle: the future active [**futurus**]. It does not have a present active participle.)

9. Because an ablative absolute explains the circumstances under which the action of the main clause takes place, it can usually be translated as a subordinate clause, introduced by "when," "since," or "although." This is a smoother translation than the all-purpose formulae, "with the noun having been participled" or "with the noun participling." Consider the following examples.

Magistro docente, discipuli discebant.	When the teacher was teaching, the students were learning.
Milite morituro, puella lacrimat.	Since the soldier is about to die, the girl weeps.
Populo metu oppresso, tyrannus potestatem habebat.	Although the people were oppressed by fear, the tyrant held on to power.

10. As the above examples indicate, the **tense of the participle in the ablative absolute is relative to the tense of the main verb**. Perfect passive participles indicate action that takes place before the main verb, present participles indicate action that takes place at the same time as the main verb, etc.

Passive Periphrastic Conjugation

11. The passive periphrastic conjugation combines a **future passive participle with a conjugated form of** the verb **sum**. The participle agrees with its subject. The passive periphrastic **indicates obligation or necessity** (since the future passive participle always indicates obligation or necessity). The passive periphrastic is best illustrated by Cato the Elder's famous statement:

Carthago delenda est.	Carthage must be destroyed.

Note that **delenda** is feminine singular nominative, agreeing with **Carthago**, and that the passive periphrastic expresses the necessity of the action.

12. This construction is called "periphrastic" because it is a roundabout or indirect way of saying something (περί + φράζω or peri + phrazō in Greek - roundabout + to speak). It is called a "conjugation" because it includes a finite or conjugated form of **sum**.

13. When the agent is specified, it is put into the dative case without a preposition. This is called the **dative of agent**:

    Hoc faciendum est mihi.   This must be done by me.
    Multae res Caesari faciendae erant.   Many things had to be done by Caesar.

14. As the above example shows, **sum** does not need to be in the present tense.

15. Occasionally a passive periphrastic will be **impersonal**. In this case, there is no subject, and the participle is neuter singular.

    Currendum est gladiatori.   There must be a running by the gladiator.
                                  The gladiator must run.
    Nobis fugiendum erat.   There had to be a fleeing by us.
                                  We had to flee.

    It is sometimes better to revise the literal translation of an impersonal passive periphrastic by rephrasing it as active.

16. Note that when the passive periphrastic conjugation is put into indirect discourse, **sum** changes into an infinitive form:

    Cato dixit Carthaginem delendam esse.   Cato said that Carthage must be destroyed.

Lingua Latina Ubique

Mutatis mutandis - With the things changed that need to be changed. This Medieval Latin phrase is used when someone is stressing the likeness between two things, as a way of acknowledging that there are some differences between the two things as well as similarities.

For example: "Teaching Latin in England is very much like teaching Latin in the United States, *mutatis mutandis*." By using this phrase, the speaker emphasizes the similarities in teaching Latin in the two countries, while acknowledging that there are some aspects of teaching Latin in England that are quite different from teaching Latin in the United States.

Note that this phrase is an ablative absolute, made up of a perfect passive participle and a gerundive (or future passive participle) showing obligation or necessity.

Status quo: Literally, **the state in which**, i.e., **the existing state of affairs.** It is often used in the context of social or political conditions, to describe the current situation as opposed to a possible change.

For example: "In regard to raising taxes, all commission members voted to maintain the *status quo*."

Two related phrases are the **status quo ante - the state of things that existed before**, and the **status quo ante bellum - the state of things that existed before the war**.

Verbatim: This is a Medieval Latin adverb meaning **word-for-word** or **in the exact words**. For example: "This law was copied *verbatim* from the lobbyist's website."

This adverb is formed from the Latin noun **verbum**, or **word**. There are a number of other Latin adverbs that end in **-im**, including **statim - immediately; passim - scattered far and wide;** and **interim - meanwhile, in the meantime.**

CHAPTER 4

Exercises

A. Translate the following sentences that include ablative absolutes.

1. Gladiatore necato, populus diu clamabat.

2. Servo ab domino vocato, omnes mirati sunt quae causa esset.

3. Exercitu coacto, Caesar cum hostibus pugnabat.

4. Igne viso, omnes liberi territi sunt.

5. Orator, signo ab senatu dato, incepit orare.

6. Duce bono, milites bene pugnaverunt.

7. Equo in urbem tracto, Graeci Troiam ceperunt.

8. Isto tenente potestatem, civile bellum timeo.

B. Translate the following sentences that include the passive periphrastic conjugation.

1. Scisne omnia quae tibi scienda sunt?

2. Cista servis movenda erit.

3. Quid faciendum est?

4. Pecuniae cupiditas fugienda est.

5. Oraculum Atheniensibus consulendum erit.

6. Nostra patria nobis amanda est.

7. Morandum tibi non est.

8. Hic ludus gladiatorius omnibus spectandus erat.

9. Discipuli magistris laudandi sunt.

10. Ad oppidum mihi ambulandum erat.

ABLATIVE ABSOLUTES; PASSIVE PERIPHRASTIC CONJUGATION

C. Translate the following English sentences into Latin.

1. With the soldiers having been collected, the general conquered the enemy.

2. With the city having been founded, a king had to be chosen.

3. After the terrible omen was seen (use ablative absolute), the oracle had to be consulted.

4. A long letter will have to be written by the girl.

5. After the crime had been committed, Hercules had to perform twelve labors. (Use ablative absolute and the passive periphrastic.)

5

Infinitives and Indirect Discourse

Infinitives

1. Latin has **six infinitives** (three active and three passive), formed as follows.

tense	active	passive
pres	present stem + **-re** (= 2nd principal part)	1st, 2nd, 4th conjugations: present stem + **-ri** 3rd conjugation: present stem + **-i**
perf	perfect stem + **-isse**	perfect passive participle + **esse**
fut	future active participle + **esse**	supine in accusative + **īrī**

2. Here are the six infinitives of **agō, agere, ēgī, āctum**:

tense	active	passive
pres	**agere,** to do	**agī,** to be done
perf	**ēgisse,** to have done	**āctus, -a, -um esse,** to have been done
fut	**āctūrus, -a, -um esse,** to be about to do, to be going to do	**āctum īrī,** to be about to be done, to be going to be done

3. To find the **present stem**, take the **present active infinitive** (second principal part) and **drop the -re**.

4. To find the **perfect stem**, take the **perfect active first person singular** (third principal part) and **drop the final -i.**

5. The **perfect passive participle** is the fourth principal part of a verb. Note that when the perfect passive participle is part of the **perfect passive infinitive**, it will **agree with its subject in gender, number, and case.**

Infinitives and Indirect Discourse

6. Similarly, when the **future active participle** is part of the **future active infinitive**, it will **agree with its subject in gender, number, and case**.

7a. The **future passive infinitive** is not common, but since it is sometimes used, students should be familiar with it. It is made up of the **supine in the accusative case** and **iri** (the **present passive infinitive of eo** - *I go*).

7b. The **supine is a fourth declension verbal noun** (i.e., a noun formed on the base of a verb). The supine is always **neuter singular**, and it only has two cases: **accusative** and **ablative**. The accusative of the supine looks exactly like the **neuter of the perfect passive participle** (fourth principal part). However, it is actually a fourth declension noun.

7c. Since the future passive infinitive is made from the **supine** (which is a neuter noun), it **never changes its form**. In other words, the supine does **not** agree with a subject in gender, number, and case because it is a noun (not an adjective).

Indirect Discourse

8. The following sentences are **direct statements.**

   The cook is preparing the dinner.
   Caesar has a dog.
   He is a good man.

9. **Indirect statements, on the other hand, are** *reported statements.*

   He says that the cook is preparing the dinner.
   Cicero sees that Caesar has a dog.
   I believe that he is a good man.

10. In both English and Latin, **indirect statements are statements introduced by words of thinking, saying, knowing, or believing.**

11. In English, we usually signal an indirect statement by making it into a subordinate clause introduced by the conjunction *that*. Occasionally, however, we signal an indirect statement by **changing the subject of the indirect statement into the accusative case and changing the verb to the infinitive:**

    He is a good man. (direct statement)
    I believe **that he is** a good man. (indirect statement with the conjunction *that*)
    I believe **him to be** a good man. (indirect statement with accusative/infinitive construction)

Chapter 5

In the last example, the **subject** of the indirect statement is changed to the **accusative case** (**he** → **him**) and the **verb** is changed to the **infinitive** (**is** → **to be**). The meaning of the last two examples is the same.

12. **Latin *always* uses the accusative/infinitive method of changing a direct statement into an indirect statement.** Study the following examples of direct and indirect statements.

Coquus parat cenam.	The cook is preparing the dinner.
Dicit coquum parare cenam.	He says that the cook is preparing the dinner.
Caesar habet canem.	Caesar has a dog.
Cicero cognoscit Caesarem habere canem.	Cicero knows that Caesar has a dog.
Is est bonus homo.	He is a good man.
Credo eum esse bonum hominem.	I believe him to be a good man.

    In each Latin sentence, when a direct statement is changed to an indirect statement, **the subject of the indirect statement is changed to the accusative case, and the verb is changed to the infinitive.**

13. In an indirect statement, the **tense of the infinitive is relative to the tense of the introductory verb**. A **present infinitive = same time** as the introductory verb. A **perfect infinitive = time before** the main verb. A **future infinitive = time after** the main verb.

    Consider the following examples.

Dicit coquum parare cenam.	He says that the cook is preparing the dinner.
Dixit coquum parare cenam.	He said that the cook was preparing the dinner.
Dicit coquum paravisse cenam.	He says that the cook prepared the dinner.
Dixit coquum paravisse cenam.	He said that the cook had prepared the dinner.
Dicit coquum paraturum esse cenam.	He says that the cook will prepare the dinner.
Dixit coquum paraturum esse cenam.	He said that the cook would prepare the dinner.

14. Latin uses the **reflexive pronoun** to indicate that the **subject of the direct statement is the same as the subject of the indirect statement**. Study the following examples.

    Cicero knows that Caesar has a dog.
    Cicero cognoscit Caesarem habere canem.
    Caesar knows that he (Caesar) has a dog.
    Caesar cognoscit se habere canem.

    Note: In Latin, an indirect statement **always** includes the reflexive pronoun if the subject of the direct statement is the same as the indirect statement.

INFINITIVES AND INDIRECT DISCOURSE

15. Note that in indirect discourse, when a verb is put into the infinitive, the object of the verb remains the same. For example:

Coquus parat cenam.   The cook is preparing the dinner.
Dicit coquum parare cenam.   He says that the cook is preparing the dinner.

In both sentences, the verb **parare** takes an accusative object, whether it is in a finite (**parat**) or infinitive (**parare**) form. The object of the verb does not change when the verb is put into the infinitive.

Lingua Latina Ubique

Ad hominem - Against the person. This Latin term is short for **argumentum ad hominem**, or **an argument against the person.** It refers to a rhetorical strategy in which the speaker attacks the character of the person making an argument rather than addressing the substance of the argument itself.

For example, if a mother tells her son to quit smoking because smoking is unhealthy, the son could reply that the mother is a smoker herself. This is an **ad hominem** argument because it does not contradict the mother's point, that smoking is unhealthy, but it seeks to discredit the argument because of an attribute of the person who is saying it.

Per se: Although the phrase can mean **by himself, by herself,** or **by itself**, it is usually used in the sense of **by itself**, or **in and of itself**, without considering any extraneous factors.

For example: "I am not allergic to the cat *per se*, but only to a protein in the cat's saliva."

Note that **se** is the accusative of the third person reflexive pronoun.

De facto: Literally, **from the fact**, this phrase is usually translated as **in fact** or **in reality.** It usually describes what actually happens in practice, in contrast to **de jure** (**by law**), which describes what happens according to law.

For example: "Even though the legal drinking age is 21, the *de facto* drinking age is often 18 or even younger."

Semper Fidelis - Always Faithful. This has been the motto of the United States Marine Corps since 1883, although it is usually shortened to **Semper Fi** (which is not real Latin).

The US Marines are not alone in adopting this motto. **Semper Fidelis** has been the motto of various European towns and families since the Middle Ages.

Chapter 5

Exercises

A. Translate the following sentences. Remember that in indirect statement, the tense of the infinitive is relative to the tense of the introductory verb.

1. Dicit Herculem necare leonem.

2. Dixit Herculem necare leonem.

3. Dixit Herculem necavisse leonem.

4. Dicit Herculem necaturum esse leonem.

5. Dixit Herculem necaturum esse leonem.

6. Puer dicit puellam natare ad insulam.

7. Puer dixit puellam natare ad insulam.

8. Puer dixit puellam natavisse ad insulam.

9. Puer dicit puellam nataturam esse ad insulam.

10. Scio librum legi a puero.

11. Scivi librum legi a puero.

12. Scivi librum lectum esse a puero.

13. Scivi librum lectum iri a puero.

14. Servus nuntiavit cenam coctam esse.

15. Credo oratores mox locuturos esse.

B. Translate the following sentences.

1. Audimus liberos ad ludum ire.

2. Mea mater dixit iter esse longum.

3. Liberi sciunt magistrum ad ludum venturum esse.

4. Dux dixit se pugnam victurum esse.

5. Dux dixit se pugnam vixisse.

6. Rex dicit cibum populo datum iri.

7. Milites sciunt se semper fideles futuros esse.

8. Viri sciunt suas uxores semper fideles futuras esse.

9. Rex dicit deos semper laudatum iri.

10. Populus discit Caesarem bellum civile gessisse.

11. Rex scit oraculum consulendum esse.

12. Rex scivit oraculos consultum iri.

13. Rex scivit se oraculum consulturum esse.

C. Translate the following English sentences into Latin.

1. I thought that father would send the letter.

2. Augustus announced that all the temples had been repaired.

3. The general said that the slaves would be freed.

4. The general said that he would free the slaves.

5. The parents said that their son was sleeping.

6

Gerunds and Gerundives

Gerunds

1. A gerund is a verbal noun (i.e., a noun formed from a verb). It is always a **second declension neuter noun, it is always singular**, and it has only four cases: genitive, dative, accusative, and ablative (no nominative). The verbal noun in the nominative case is supplied by the infinitive.

2. The gerund is formed from the **present stem + -ndum**, and it is translated as **"verb-ing,"** just like the gerund in English. Consider the following examples.

    laudandum - praising
    laudandi - of praising
    laudando - by praising
    canendum - singing
    canendi - of singing
    canendo - by singing
    vivendum - living
    vivendi - of living
    vivendo - by living

3. The gerund can be used as a noun in a sentence in any function except the subject, but, like a verb, it can be modified by an adverb and (in the genitive and ablative cases) it can take a direct object. Consider the following examples.

ars scribendi	the art of writing
ars vivendi	the art of living
modus vivendi	manner of living
Magister scit artem vivendi bene.	The teacher knows the art of living well.
Docendo discimus.	We learn by teaching.
Docendo discipulos discimus.	We learn by teaching students.

amor canendi	the love of singing
Puella habit amorem carmina canendi.	The girl has a love of singing songs.

Note that in both English and Latin, words such as "writing," "living," "teaching," and "singing" are nouns, even though they are formed from verbs and still keep some of their verbal qualities. In Latin, only the genitive and ablative of the gerund will usually take a direct object.

4. As noted above, the nominative case of the verbal noun is supplied by the present active infinitive, as in the following examples.

Errare est humanum.	To err is human.
Ars poetica non omnia dicere.	The art of poetry is not to say everything. (Horace)

5. The gerund is also used in the accusative case with the preposition **ad** and in the genitive (postpositively) with the prepositions **causā** and **gratiā** to show purpose, as in the following examples.

Ludum aedificavit discendi gratiā	He built a school for the sake of learning.
Philosophos quaesivit ad audiendum.	He sought the philosophers for the sake of listening.
Ad ludum venit legendi causā.	He went to school for the purpose of reading.

Gerundives

6. The **gerundive** is another name for the **future passive participle**. It is formed from **the present stem + -ndus, -nda, -ndum**; it agrees with its subject in gender, number, and case; and it expresses obligation or necessity.

7. The gerundive looks like a gerund, and it has some uses that are similar to the gerund, but the **gerundive (like all participles) is an adjective** while the **gerund is a neuter singular noun.**

8. Gerundives are used in **three main constructions**.

   (1) The **passive periphrastic conjugation.** This is discussed in Chapter 4.
   (2) The gerundive **used idiomatically in place of a gerund with an object,** discussed below.
   (3) The gerundive used in the accusative with **ad**, and in the genitive with **causā** and **gratiā** to **show purpose.** This construction is exactly the same as **ad, causā, and gratiā with the gerund.**

CHAPTER 6

9. Because the Romans did not like to use the gerund with a direct object, they frequently used an idiomatic construction with the gerundive instead. An **idiomatic construction** is one that is quirky and, in some ways, defies logic; it usually **cannot be translated literally**. For example, in English we use the idiomatic expression "to take a shower," even though we are not actually "taking" the shower to a different location.

The Romans frequently used an idiomatic construction with the gerundive in place of a gerund with a direct object. This idiomatic gerundive should not be translated literally. In the following examples, the **sentences in A use a gerund with a direct object**, while the **sentences in B say the same thing using the preferred gerundive**.

A. Puer habet studium libros legendi
B. Puer habet studium librorum legendorum.

The boy has a desire for reading books.
The boy has a desire for books to be read. (literally)
The boy has a desire for reading books. (idiomatically)

A. Dux spem servandi populum habuit.
B. Dux spem servandi populi habuit.

The general had a hope of saving the people.
The general had a hope of the people to be saved. (literally)
The general had a hope of saving the people. (idiomatically)

A. Operam dat servando populum.
B. Operam dat populo servando.

He gives attention to saving the people.
He gives attention to the people to be saved. (literally)
He gives attention to saving the people. (idiomatically)

A. Venit ad legendum libros.
B. Venit ad libros legendos.

He came for the purpose of reading books.
He came for the purpose of books to be read. (literally)
He came for the purpose of reading books. (idiomatically)

In the above "B" examples, the **gerundives** (as adjectives) agree with their nouns in gender, number, and case, but they **are translated idiomatically as if the nouns were their direct objects** (which in fact they are not).

10. Although gerunds and gerundives are used in similar ways, they can be distinguished as follows.

gerunds	gerundives
nouns	adjectives
neuter only	can be masculine, feminine, or neuter
singular only	can be singular or plural
genitive, accusative, dative, and ablative only (no nominative case)	can be in any case, including the nominative
DO NOT AGREE with an accompanying noun	AGREE with an accompanying noun in gender, number, and case

Lingua Latina Ubique

Some English words and expressions use gerunds or gerundives.

Agenda: Literally, **things to be done.** This is a gerundive (a future passive participle) showing obligation or necessity in the neuter nominative or accusative plural.

Memoranda: Similarly, **things to be remembered.**

Propaganda: From the Latin verb, **propago, propagare - to spread, increase,** or **propagate**, this word means **things to be spread or propagated.**

Modus vivendi - Mode of living or **way of life.** It is usually used to describe a particular lifestyle.
    For example: "Buying groceries online has become my new *modus vivendi*."
    Note that **modus** is a second declension noun and **vivendi** is a gerund (noun) in the genitive case: **mode of living.**

Exercises

A. Translate the following sentences and identify the gerunds and/or gerundives.

1. Legati ad pacem petendam venerunt.

2. Discimus libris legendis.

3. Discimus legendo.

4. Coniurationem nascentem non credendo corroboraverunt. (Cicero)

5. Aliquas scientias discimus agendo. (Aristotle)

6. Ista fabula narranda est.

7. Ancilla ad hortum laborandi causa ambulat.

8. Ancilla ad hortum laborum faciendorum causa ambulat.

9. Consulendis oraculis rex multum didicit.

10. Negotium inveniendae statuae magistro suscipiendum est.

B. Translate the following sentences and identify the gerunds and/or gerundives.

1. Captivus in via currens spem fugiendi invenit.

2. Orator loquendo publice suam sententiam narrare potest.

3. Orator ad forum vēnit ad suam sententiam narrandam.

4. Orator ad forum vēnit suae sententiae narrandae gratiā.

5. Bene pugnando milites hostes vicerunt.

6. Ad urbem tibi ambulandum erit.

7. Agricolae arandis agris laboraverunt, milites autem pugnando laboraverunt.

8. Servus ad forum mittendus est emendi cibi gratia.

9. Multum temporis consumo in libris legendis.

10. Ad eas res conficiendas homines missi sunt.

C. Translate the following English sentences into Latin, using gerunds and gerundives where appropriate.

1. By throwing javelins, the Romans conquered the enemy.

2. He was always desirous of waging war.

3. This mother has hope of seeing her son.

4. The Sabines sent ambassadors for the purpose of seeking peace. (Write two versions, one using **ad** and one using **causa** or **gratia**.)

5. You must read these books. (Use passive periphrastic.)

6. The soldier was sent for fighting. (Use **ad**.)

7

Subjunctive Forms

1. The **mood** of a Latin verb indicates the **mode** or **manner of expression**. There are **three moods** in Latin: **indicative, imperative, and subjunctive.** (The infinitive form of a verb is sometimes incorrectly referred to as a mood.)

2. The **indicative** expresses **reality** or a **statement of fact** (which can be true or false). The **imperative** expresses a **command**. The **subjunctive** expresses an **idea** as something **conceived of** or **thought about**, but not necessarily true or false.

3. The word "**subjunctive**" means "**joined to**" or "**dependent**." And in fact **most uses of the subjunctive are in dependent clauses** (rather than main or independent clauses). However, the subjunctive is also used in a few types of **independent or main clauses**.

4. **This chapter** will review the **forms** of the subjunctive. **Chapter 8** will discuss the **independent uses** of the subjunctive, and **subsequent chapters** will deal with the *many* uses of the subjunctive in **dependent clauses.**

5. The **subjunctive mood** has only **four tenses: present, imperfect, perfect, and pluperfect.** The subjunctives of these four tenses occur in both the active and passive voices. (There are no future or future perfect subjunctives.)

6. The **present subjunctive** (both active and passive) is formed by **changing the characteristic vowel** of the present stem (the present active infinitive minus **-re**). The first conjugation changes from **a** to **e**. The second conjugation changes from **long e** to **ea**. The third changes from **short e** to **a**. And the fourth and third **io** conjugations change from **i** to **ia**. Thus, in all conjugations **other than the first, a is the characteristic vowel** of the present subjunctive.

   These changes can easily be remembered from the following sentence.

W<u>e</u>	f<u>ear</u>	<u>a</u>	l<u>ia</u>r.
1st	2nd	3rd	4th + 3rd io

7. **Present Subjunctives:** Please learn the present subjunctives of the following paradigm verbs:

   1st conjugation: amō, amāre, amāvī, amātum - to love
   2nd conjugation: moneō, monēre, monuī, monitum - to warn, advise
   3rd conjugation: dūcō, dūcere, dūxī, ductum - to lead
   3rd -io conjugation: capiō, capere, cēpī, captum - to take, capture
   4th conjugation: audiō, audīre, audīvī, audītum - to hear

Perfect Subjunctives

conj	active	passive
1st	amem, amēs, amet, amēmus, amētis, ament	amer, amēris or -re, amētur, amēmur, amēminī, amentur
2nd	moneam, moneās, moneat, moneāmus, moneātis, moneant	monear, moneāris or -re, moneātur, moneāmur, moneāminī, moneantur
3rd	dūcam, dūcās, dūcat, dūcāmus, dūcātis, dūcant	dūcar, dūcāris, dūcātur, dūcāmur, dūcāminī, dūcantur
3rd -io	capiam, capiās, capiat, capiāmus, capiātis, capiant	capiar, capiāris or -re, capiātur, capiāmur, capiāminī, capiantur
4th	audiam, audiās, audiat, audiāmus, audiātis, audiant	audiar, audiāris or -re, audiātur, audiāmur, audiāminī, audiantur

8. The **imperfect subjunctive** (both active and passive) is formed by adding the **personal endings directly on to the present active infinitive**.

Imperfect Subjunctives

conj	active	passive
1st	amārem, amārēs, amāret, amārēmus, amārētis, amārent	amārer, amārēris or -re, amārētur, amārēmur, amārēminī, amārentur
2nd	monērem, monērēs, monēret, monērēmus, monērētis, monērent	monērer, monērēris or -re, monērētur, monērēmur, monērēminī, monērentur
3rd	dūcerem, dūcerēs, dūceret, dūcerēmus, dūcerētis, dūcerent	dūcerer, dūcerēris or -re, dūcerētur, dūcerēmur, dūcerēminī, dūcerentur
3rd -io	caperem, caperēs, caperet, caperēmus, caperētis, caperent	caperer, caperēris or -re, caperētur, caperēmur, caperēminī, caperentur
4th	audīrem, audīrēs, audīret, audīrēmus, audīrētis, audīrent	audīrer, audīrēris or -re, audīrētur, audīrēmur, audīrēminī, audīrentur

9. **The present subjunctive of sum is irregular.** It is presented here along with the imperfect, perfect, and pluperfect subjunctives (which are regular):

Subjunctive Forms

Present and Imperfect Subjunctives of sum

person/#	pres	imperf	perf	pluperf
sing 1	sim	essem	fuerim	fuissem
2	sīs	essēs	fuerīs	fuissēs
3	sit	esset	fuerit	fuisset
plu 1	sīmus	essēmus	fuerīmus	fuissēmus
2	sītis	essētis	fuerītis	fuissētis
3	sint	essent	fuerint	fuissent

10. The **perfect active subjunctive** is formed by adding **-eri + personal endings to the perfect stem**. (The perfect stem is the first person **perfect indicative** without the final -**i**.) The **perfect passive subjunctive** is a compound tense, formed from the **perfect passive participle and the present subjunctive of sum**. Note that the perfect passive participle agrees with its subject in gender, number, and case.

Perfect Subjunctives

conj	active	passive
1st	amāverim, amāverīs, amāverit, amāverīmus, amāverītis, amāverint	amātus sim, amātus sīs, amātus sit, amātī sīmus, amātī sītis, amātī sint
2nd	monuerim, monuerīs, monuerit, monuerīmus, monuerītis, monuerint	monitus sim, monitus sīs, monitus sit, monitī sīmus, monitī sītis, monitī sint
3rd	dūxerim, dūxerīs, dūxerit, dūxerīmus, dūxerītis, dūxerint	ductus sim, ductus sīs, ductus sit, ductī sīmus, ductī sītis, ductī sint
3rd -io	cēperim, cēperīs, cēperit, cēperīmus, cēperītis, cēperint	captus sim, captus sīs, captus sit, captī sīmus, captī sītis, captī sint
4th	audīverim, audīverīs, audīverit, audīverīmus, audīverītis, audīverint	audītus sim, audītus sīs, audītus sit, audītī sīmus, audītī sītis, audītī sint

11. The **pluperfect active subjunctive** is formed by adding the **personal endings to the perfect active infinitive**. The **pluperfect passive subjunctive** is a compound tense, formed from the **perfect passive participle and the imperfect subjunctive of sum**. Note that the perfect passive participle agrees with its subject in gender, number, and case.

Pluperfect Subjunctives

conj	active	passive
1st	amāvissem, amāvissēs, amāvisset, amāvissēmus, amāvissētis, amāvissent	amātus essem, amātus essēs, amātus esset, amātī essēmus, amātī essētis, amātī essent
2nd	monuissem, monuissēs, monuisset, monuissēmus, monuissētis, monuissent	monitus essem, monitus essēs, monitus esset, monitī essēmus, monitī essētis, monitī essent
3rd	dūxissem, dūxissēs, dūxisset, dūxissēmus, dūxissētis, dūxissent	ductus essem, ductus essēs, ductus esset, ductī essēmus, ductī essētis, ductī essent
3rd io	cēperīm, cēperīs, cēperit, cēperīmus, cēperītis, cēperint	captus essem, captus essēs, captus esset, captī essēmus, captī essētis, captī essent
4th	audīvissem, audīvissēs, audīvisset, audīvissēmus, audīvissētis, audīvissent	audītus essem, audītus essēs, audītus esset, audītī essēmus, audītī essētis, audītī essent

Lingua Latina Ubique

Sui generis - Of his/her/its own kind. This phrase is usually used to mean that someone or something is **in a class by itself** or **unique**. This term can be applied to a book or film that does not fit into a standard genre, and it has been applied to unusual political entities (such as Vatican City) which do not fit into the normal category of nation-state.

Ad hoc - To this or **for this (specific purpose).** This phrase is used to describe a committee or other group that is created for a specific task and that will be dissolved once that task has been completed.

For example: "An ad hoc committee was created to plan the twenty-five-year celebration."

Vice versa - With the order changed or **in reverse order.**

For example: "Water can be changed to ice and *vice versa*." Or: "He doesn't believe her and *vice versa*," i.e., she doesn't believe him either.

Vice is the ablative singular of a feminine noun meaning **change, exchange,** or **interchange**, while **versa** is the feminine perfect passive participle of **verto, to turn back, turn around, change,** or **reverse**. So the phrase is an ablative absolute meaning **with the exchange having been turned** or **with the exchange having been made**.

Referendum - (Something) to be referred (to the people for a vote). A **referendum** is a proposal that is decided by a direct vote of the citizens, rather than being voted on by an elected representative. It is sometimes called a ballot measure, a proposition, or a plebiscite.

Subjunctive Forms

This word is the neuter singular of the gerundive of **refero, referre - to bring back,** or **carry back**.

Because it is a gerundive, like **agenda** and **memoranda** (discussed in Chapter 6), **referendum** implies obligation or necessity.

Although this word is usually used in the singular, the Latin plural, **referenda**, is sometimes used as well.

The English word **plebiscite** is from the Latin **plebiscitum**, a decree of the **Concilium Plebis** (Plebeian Council). **Plebiscita** were originally binding only on plebians, but eventually (in 287 BCE) they became binding on all Romans, thus formally ending the Conflict of the Orders.

Exercises

A. Change the following present active indicative verbs to the corresponding subjunctive active forms.

	pres indic	pres subj	imperf subj	perf subj	pluperf subj
1	laudat				
2	moneo				
3	ducimus				
4	veniunt				
5	facitis				
6	amas				
7	timent				
8	vincit				
9	paretis				
10	oramus				

B. Change the following present passive indicative verbs to the corresponding subjunctive passive forms.

	pres indic	pres subj	imperf subj	perf subj	pluperf subj
1	laudatur				
2	moneor				
3	ducimur				
4	veniuntur				
5	capimini				
6	amaris				
7	finior				
8	vincitur				
9	manemini				
10	oramur				

C. Rewrite the following sentences, changing the verbs into the same tense of the subjunctive.

1. Hoc castellum a barbaris oppugnatur.

2. Quis cum legato appropinquavit?

3. Ager a hostibus vastatus est.

4. Milites a Caesare laudantur.

5. Captivi saepe cibum postulabant.

6. Copiae nostrae a sociis laudatae erant.

8

Independent Uses of the Subjunctive

1. There are **five uses of the subjunctive in independent (main) clauses: deliberative, hortatory, jussive, optative, and potential**.

2. The **deliberative** subjunctive usually occurs in the **first person** (singular and plural) to **express a deliberation**, frequently in the form of a question. The negative is **non**. The present tense is used to express a present deliberation, and the imperfect is used to express a past deliberation. Occasionally the deliberative subjunctive occurs in the third person.

    Examples:
Quid faciam?	What should I do?
Quid facerem?	What was I to do?
Nonne hunc librum legeremus?	Were we not to read this book?
Concedamus huic?	Should we yield to this man?

3. The **hortatory subjunctive** usually occurs in the **first person plural**, and in the **present tense**. The negative is **ne**. The hortatory subjunctive expresses an **exhortation**. It is usually translated into English with "**let us**," as in "Let us sing."

    Examples:
Nunc eamus.	Let us go now.
Pugnemus pro patria.	Let us fight for our country.
Ne desperemus.	Let us not despair.
Nostros amicos moneamus.	Let us warn our friends.

4. The **jussive subjunctive** usually occurs in the **third person** (singular and plural) and in the **present tense**. It expresses a **command**, and is usually translated with "**let him**," "**let her**," or "**let them**." The negative is **ne**.

Examples:
Mater fabulam dicat.	Let mother tell the story.
Improbi secedant.	Let the wicked men depart.
Cibus nunc ne coquatur.	Let the food not be cooked now.
Tres legiones in castris maneant.	Let three legions remain in camp.

5. The **optative subjunctive** expresses a **wish**. It is frequently (but not always) introduced by **utinam**, "would that," or "if only." The **present subjunctive** is used for a **present or future wish**; in this case, the wish is conceived of as **possible**. The **imperfect subjunctive** is used to express regret that something is not the case in the present (a **present contrary-to-fact wish**), and the **pluperfect subjunctive** is used to express regret that something was not the case in the past (a **past contrary-to-fact wish**). The negative is **ne**.

Examples:
Utinam milites nunc auxilium adducant.	If only the soldiers would bring help now.
Utinam coquus cibum coquat.	If only the cook would cook dinner.
Utinam istud ex animo diceres.	If only you were saying that in earnest. (But I believe you are not saying it in earnest.)
Utinam ne hostes venissent.	Would that the enemy had not come. (But the enemy did come.)

6. The **potential subjunctive** expresses a **possibility**. The negative is **non**. The potential subjunctive can be translated with the English auxiliaries "**may**," "**might**," "**should**," "**could**," or "**would**," depending on the context.

Examples:
Nolim urbem deleri.	I would not wish the city to be destroyed.
Aliquis dicat hunc impium esse.	Someone may say that this man is wicked.
Illum periculum facile vitare possis.	You could easily avoid that danger.
Piscemur cras.	We may go fishing tomorrow.

Lingua Latina Ubique

Caveat emptor - Let the buyer beware. This Latin phrase, which has become a proverb in English, indicates that the person who purchases something is responsible for making sure that the item actually is all that the seller claims it is.

    Example: "The website says that this purse is made of leather, but *caveat emptor*."
    Note that this phrase uses the present subjunctive of the verb **caveo, cavere**, meaning **beware, be cautious, take heed**. This phrase is a good example of the jussive use of the subjunctive.

Modus operandi - Mode of operating. This phrase, often abbreviated as **MO**, is frequently used to describe a typical way of doing something, especially of criminals.

Independent Uses of the Subjunctive

Example: "This bank robber always wears a clown mask for his heists; that's his MO."
Note that (like **vivendi** in **modus vivendi** in Chapter 6) **operandi** is a gerund (verbal noun).

Etc. (et cetera) - And the rest (of such things). This phrase comes from the Latin word **et** (**and**) and the nominative plural of **ceterum**, a neuter noun (usually used in the plural) meaning **the rest** or **the other (similar) things**.

The ancient Greeks used a similar expression: καὶ τὰ λοιπά (**kai ta loipa**) - **and the rest.**

Imprimatur - Let it be printed. In English, this is a noun meaning **sanction** or **approval**, but in Latin it is a verb. It is the third person singular, present subjunctive passive of **imprimo, imprimere, impressi, impressum - to stamp, imprint, mark**. It is a jussive subjunctive.

With the introduction of the printing press (c. 1452), this verb came to mean "to print or publish."

Imprimatur was first used by the Catholic Church, as an official stamp of approval, indicating that a work may be published.

Today it is used to signify any mark of official approval or endorsement.
Example: "The CDC put its imprimatur on this article about the origin of Covid-19."

Exercises

A. Translate each of the Latin sentences below and identify the use of the subjunctive, whether it is deliberative, hortatory, jussive, optative, or potential.

1. Ne diutius in hoc loco maneamus.

2. Utinam te numquam vidissem.

3. Ne pater pereat.

4. Tradamne patriam?

5. Proficiscar cras?

6. Videas maiores naves in portu.

7. Semper amicos nostros defendamus.

8. Centurio legionem ex castris educat.

9. Imperator auxilium mittat.

10. Utinam imperator auxilium mittat.

11. Utinam frater meus me nunc videre posset.

12. Utinam illi peregrini in patria sua nunc essent.

13. Ille homo propter facinora sua ex urbe expellatur.

14. Imperator comites deligat.

15. Utinam legio impetum barbarorum diutius sustinuisset.

B. Translate each of the Latin sentences below and identify the use of the subjunctive, whether it is deliberative, hortatory, jussive, optative, or potential.

1. Auxilium a Caesare quaeramus, quod hostes magnis cum copiis appropinquant.

2. Praemium offerre velim.

3. Quis Romam in bello vincat?

4. Arenturne agri nunc aut serius?

5. Utinam liberi nunc dormiant.

6. Romanorum historiam nunc legere malim.

7. Ne sedeat Caesar sub hac arbore.

8. Navigem hodie aut cras?

9. Utinam e nostra patria ne exivissemus!

10. Oraculum consulamus.

11. Cibumne nunc coquam?

12. Ex hoc malo loco exeamus.

13. Quis meliorem librum legat?

14. Deos patriae laudemus?

15. Deos patriae laudemus!

Independent Uses of the Subjunctive

C. Translate the following English sentences into Latin, and identify the type of subjunctive being used.

1. Let us leave our books in this safe place.

2. Do not let the general fortify this camp in this dangerous place.

3. If only we had never seen this city!

4. Should I announce the oracle or keep quiet?

5. This craftsman might build a better ship.

9

Sequence of Tenses; Purpose and Result Clauses

1. As noted above, **most of the uses of the subjunctive are in subordinate (dependent) clauses**. In fact, the name "subjunctive" means "subordinate." The rest of this book will be devoted to the uses of the subjunctive in subordinate clauses.

Sequence of Tenses

2. The term **"sequence of tenses"** refers to the rules that govern **what tenses of the subjunctive in a subordinate clause are to be used after what tenses of the main verb** (which is usually, though not always, in the indicative). In order to understand these rules, you must first learn the terms **primary and secondary tenses**.

3. **Primary Tense: A primary tense refers to the present or future**. There are four primary tenses in Latin:

   present: refers to present time
   future: refers to future time
   perfect: when it is a true perfect, that is, **a present state that is caused by a past action**. In English we call this tense a "present perfect"; it is usually translated with "has" or "have." For example: I have eaten breakfast this morning.
   future perfect: refers to something that will have happened at a future time. For example: He will have already eaten dinner by the time they arrive.

4. **Secondary Tense: A secondary tense refers to the past.** There are three secondary tenses in Latin:

   imperfect: refers to a repeated, habitual, or ongoing event in the past
   perfect: **when it is used as a simple past**, that is, a one-time event that occurred in the past. For example: I ate breakfast this morning.

pluperfect: refers to an event in the past that occurred before another past event. For example: I had already eaten breakfast when my colleague offered me a doughnut.

5. Please memorize the following table.

Sequence of Tenses

	main verb	subord subj
primary sequence	primary tense	present subj - same time or time after perfect subj - time before
secondary sequence	secondary tense	imperf subj - same time or time after pluperf subj - time before

6. **Primary Sequence:** After a main verb in a primary tense, the present subjunctive shows action occurring at the same time as the main verb or time after (future time), while the perfect subjunctive shows action that has already occurred.

   I sing a song so as to please my mother.
   Cano carmen ut **placeam** matrem.

   In this sentence, a main verb in the present (primary tense) is followed by a **present subjunctive** to show action that happens at the **same time or time after (future time)**.

   I know where the thief put the gold.
   Scio quo fur **posuerit** aurum.

   In this sentence, a main verb in the present (primary tense) is followed by a **perfect subjunctive** to show action that **has already occurred** before the action of the main verb **(past time)**.

7. **Secondary Sequence:** After a main verb in a secondary (past) tense, the **imperfect subjunctive** shows action occurring at the **same time as the main verb or time after**, while the **pluperfect subjunctive** shows action that has **already occurred (past time)**.

   I sang a song in order to please my mother.
   Cantavi carmen ut **placerem** matrem.

   In this sentence, a main verb in the perfect (secondary tense) is followed by an **imperfect subjunctive** to show action that happens at the **same time** or a future time.

57

I knew where the thief had put the gold.
Scivi quo fur **posuisset** aurum.

In this sentence, a main verb in the perfect (secondary tense) is followed by a **pluperfect subjunctive** to show action that **has already occurred** before the main verb takes place.

Nota Bene (note well): In the above table, a subjunctive describing action that occurs at the **same time or time after** the main verb denotes an **incomplete action** (that is, an action that has not been completed at the time when the main verb takes place).

Similarly, a subjunctive describing action that has **already occurred** before the main verb takes place denotes a **completed action**.

Purpose Clauses

8. A purpose clause is a type of dependent clause. To show purpose, the Romans used **ut** followed by the **subjunctive**. To show a **negative purpose,** the Romans used **ne** followed by the **subjunctive**.

    Examples:

Hoc facio ut vos iuvem.	I do this in order that I may help you.
	(primary sequence: present subjunctive showing same or future time.)
Hoc feci ut vos iuvarem.	I did this in order that I might help you.
	(secondary sequence: imperfect subjunctive showing same or future time.)
Hoc facio ut urbem capiam.	I do this in order that I may take the city.
	(primary sequence: present subjunctive showing same or future time.)
Hoc feci ut urbem caperem.	I did this in order that I might take the city.
	(secondary sequence: imperfect subjunctive showing same or future time.)
Hoc facio ne capiar.	I do this in order that I may not be captured.
	(primary sequence: present subjunctive showing same or future time.)
Hoc feci ne caperer.	I did this in order that I might not be captured.
	(secondary sequence: imperfect subjunctive showing same or future time.)

9. Note that **a purpose clause tends to look toward the future**, so there are no examples of purpose clauses showing past time (or completed action).

10. Note that **Latin does not use the infinitive to show purpose**, as we do in English. In English, we can say, "I do this to capture the city." But Latin uses **ut** or **ne** plus the **subjunctive** to show purpose.

Result Clauses

11. While a purpose clause shows the **intended purpose** or reason for an action (whether or not the intended purpose actually occurred), **a result clause shows the result of an action** (whether or not the result was intended).

    English Examples:
    Purpose clause: I sang a song so as to please my mother.
      This clause shows the singer's purpose or intention. We don't know whether or not the mother was actually pleased. (Maybe she hated the song, but the speaker's **purpose** was to please her.)

    Result clause: I sang a song with the result that my mother was pleased.
      This clause shows the result of the action. (Maybe the speaker's purpose was to please herself, but the **result** was that the mother was pleased.)

    In English, we often express both purpose and result clauses with "so that," which obscures the difference between them.

12. The Romans expressed a **result clause** with **ut** plus the subjunctive. They expressed a negative result with **ut non** plus the subjunctive.

    Examples:

Via tam angusta est ut pauca plaustra ire possint.	The road is so narrow that few carts can pass. (primary sequence: present subjunctive showing same time or time after)
Tam strenue laboravit ut urbem servaret.	He worked so hard that as a result he saved the city. (secondary sequence: imperfect subjunctive showing same time or time after)
Ita benigne dixit ut non eos offenderet.	He spoke so kindly that he did not offend them. (secondary sequence: imperfect subjunctive showing same time or time after)

13. As the above examples show, the **clause before the result clause often has a word meaning "so,"** which helps to signal that a result clause will follow. These words include **tam** (so), **ita** (so), **tantus, -a, -um** (so great), and **talis, -e** (of such a sort).

14. Like a purpose clause, **a result clause tends to look toward the future**, so there are few examples of result clauses showing past time (or completed action).

Lingua Latina Ubique

These terms and abbreviations used to be common in scholarly writing and you will still see them in older books. Can you think of any others?

id. (idem): From the Latin **idem, eadem, idem - the same.** This word is used when several works by the same author are cited successively. It refers to a different book by the same author that was cited in the previous note.

ibid. (ibidem) - In the same place, in that very place. This word refers to the same author and work that was cited in the previous note.

et al. (et alii) - Et alii (and other people). This expression is used to describe books or articles with multiple authors. Frequently the first two or three authors are listed by name, and then **et al.** is added to show that there are additional authors.

loc. cit. (loco citato) - In the place cited. This term is used with an author's name, to denote the same work and page by an author as was previously cited.
    Example: If an earlier note refers to "Rudyard Kipling, *The Jungle Book*, page 127," a later note might read, "Kipling, *loc. cit.*," which would also refer to page 127 of the *Jungle Book*.

op. cit. (opere citato) - In the work cited. This abbreviation, also used with an author's name, refers to the same work by an author as was previously cited, but a different page. So, if an earlier note refers to "Rudyard Kipling, *The Jungle Book*, page 127," a later note might read, "Kipling, *op. cit.*, p. 56," which would refer to *The Jungle Book*, page 56.

cf. (confer) - Compare or **see, by way of comparison.** This is the second person singular imperative form of the verb **confero, conferre - to compare.** This scholarly term is sometimes misused to mean **see, for example**, but in its correct use it means **compare**.

i.e. (id est) - That is, or **in other words.** Do not confuse with **e.g. (exempli gratiā) - for example** (discussed in Chapter 13).

Sequence of Tenses; Purpose and Result Clauses

Exercises

A. Translate the following sentences and state whether each one is a purpose or result clause, whether it is in primary or secondary sequence, and whether the action of the dependent clause occurs at the same time or after the main verb (incomplete action) or before the main verb (past or completed action).

1. Milites sunt tam fortes ut interficiant multos hostes.

2. Milites erant tam fortes ut interficerent multos hostes.

3. Cicero vult legere multos libros ut discat multa.

4. Cicero voluit legere multos libros ut disceret multa.

5. Ista urbs est tanta magna ut amittamus nostram viam.

6. Ista urbs erat tanta magna ut amitteremus nostram viam.

7. Cognovi bene istam urbem ut non amitterem meam viam.

8. Puer vult tacere ne turbet dormientem infantem.

9. Puer tantum constrepuit ut infans suscitaretur ex somno.

10. Ad ludum ambulemus ut fabulam magistri audiamus.

B. Translate the following sentences and state whether each one is a purpose or result clause, whether it is in primary or secondary sequence, and whether the action of the dependent clause occurs at the same time or after the main verb (incomplete action) or before the main verb (past or completed action).

1. Ad ludum ambulavimus ut fabulam magistri audiremus.

2. Viri unum diem manere constituerunt ut forum viderent.

3. Caesar vult navigare in navibus ut ad Britanniam eat.

4. Caesar et eius milites voluerunt navigare in navibus ut ad Britanniam irent.

5. Milites Caesaris erant tam timidi ut non vellent ad Britanniam navigare.

6. Orator locutus est cum tam magna arte ut audiremus libenter.

7. Servi domo profecti sunt ut ad agros irent.

8. Poeta scribit poemata ut fiat clarus.

9. Poeta scripsit poemata tam venusta ut fieret clarus.

10. Puellae feminaeque ex urbe fugiunt ne capiantur.

C. State whether the following sentences are purpose or result and whether they are in primary or secondary sequence; then translate them.

1. The homeland of the Helvetii is so small that they want to leave it.

2. Caesar sailed to Britain in order to punish the Britons.

3. The sea was so rough that the sailors were afraid.

4. The enemy knew the terrain so well that they boldly hurled their weapons.

5. The aquilifer jumped down from the ship in order to encourage the soldiers.

10

Indirect Commands; Fear Clauses

Indirect Command

1. **A direct command** ("Shut the door") is usually expressed in Latin with the imperative mood (**Portam clauda**) or, in the third person, with the jussive subjunctive (**Portam claudet.** - Let him shut the door). **An indirect command** ("I wish that you would shut the door," "He orders his servant to shut the door," etc.) is expressed in Latin with a **request or command word and ut/ne + subjunctive.**

   Examples:

Hoc facite.	Do this. (direct command using the imperative)
Hoc faciant.	Let them do this. (direct command using the jussive subjunctive)
Imperat eis ut hoc faciant.	He orders them to do this. Literally: He orders them that they do this. (indirect command in primary sequence)
Imperavit eis ut hoc facerent.	He ordered them to do this. Literally: He ordered them that they do this. (indirect command in secondary sequence)
Petivit a nobis ne hoc faceremus.	He asked us not to do this. Literally: He asked us that we not do this. (indirect command in secondary sequence)

   Nota bene (note well): Each verb that introduces an indirect command takes either a **dative of person** (for the indirect object) or a **preposition + the ablative**. For example, **peto** and **quaero** take **ab + abl** of the personal pronoun, while **impero** and **persuadeo** take the dative personal pronoun without a preposition. These must be learned or looked up in the dictionary.

2. Two Latin verbs (**iubeo** - command, and **veto** - forbid) take an accusative infinitive construction, similar to English.

Examples:
Caesar milites facere pontem iubet.   Caesar commands his soldiers to build a bridge.
Leges nos pugnare hīc vetant.   The laws forbid us to fight here.

3. **Indirect commands are sometimes called Jussive Noun Clauses.** They are called noun clauses because the dependent clause (**ut** or **ne** + subjunctive) functions like a noun in the sentence, usually the direct object of the main verb.

For example, in the sentence, **Imperat eis ut hoc faciant** (He commands them to do this), the clause **ut hoc faciant** functions like the direct object of the main verb, **imperat**. (The personal pronoun is the indirect object.) They are called jussive noun clauses because they are noun clauses that express a command.

Fear Clauses

4. Fear clauses are somewhat counterintuitive because they take a **verb of fearing + ne + subjunctive for a *positive* fear** and a **verb of fearing + ut + subjunctive for a *negative* fear.**

Examples:
Timeo ne hostes veniant.   I fear that the enemy may come.
Timeo ut socius noster veniat.   I fear that our ally may not come.

5. The origin of this seemingly backward formation may lie in an imagined causal relationship between saying something and making it happen. (This is a type of magical thinking.) In other words, the suspicion that the very act of saying something might cause it to occur.

   So if you are afraid that the enemy might come, you don't want to say it, because that might actually make it happen. Instead, you say the opposite (**ne hostes veniant** - may the enemy not come), because saying it as a negative might actually help to prevent it from happening. So this construction may have originally been something like this:

Timeo; ne hostes veniant   I am afraid; may the enemy not come.
Timeo; socius noster veniat   I am afraid; may our ally come.

This is only a theory, of course, but it is an interesting one and it may help you to remember the construction. Just remember that you use **ne** for **something that the subject does *not* want to happen** and you use **ut** for **something that the subject *does* want to happen.**

6. Since fear clauses can describe an action that has already been completed (e.g., "She feared that the gold had been stolen"), **any tense of the subjunctive can be used in a**

fear clause, in accordance with the sequence of tenses. Please review the Sequence of Tenses table below.

Sequence of Tenses

	main verb	subord subj
primary sequence	primary tense	pres subj—same time or time after perf subj—time before
secondary sequence	secondary tense	imperf subj—same time or time after pluperf subj—time before

Lingua Latina Ubique

Ad nauseam - to the point of nausea. This phrase refers to a topic that has been discussed so extensively that people are quite literally sick of it.
 Example: "The general described his victory *ad nauseam*."
 The Latin word **nausea** originally referred specifically to seasickness, and thus it is related to **navis, -is, f - ship** and **nauta, -ae, m - sailor**.

Data - discrete units of information, especially facts or statistics, that have been gathered together for reference or analysis.
 The word is the nominative plural of the neuter noun **datum - that which is given**, derived from the perfect passive participle of **do, dare - to give**.
 Note that the English noun is plural.

Media - the means of mass communication, such as radio, television, and the internet, especially social media.
 The word is the nominative plural of the neuter noun, **medium - the middle, the center, intervening space**.
 Similar to **data**, **media** is a plural noun.

Alma mater - nurturing mother. This expression is commonly used to refer to the college or university that someone attended or graduated from. It is connected to the word **alumnus** or **alumna** - "one who has been nurtured," to refer to a graduate or former student of a university.
 In classical Latin, the term **alma mater** was sometimes used to refer to a mother goddess, such as Ceres or Cybele. Lucretius refers to the earth itself as an **alma mater** in book 2 of his *De Rerum Natura*:

Chapter 10

Denique caelesti sumus omnes semine oriundi;
omnibus ille idem pater est, unde alma liquentis
umoris guttas mater cum terra recepit (2.991–93).

And finally, we are all born from heavenly seed;
we all have the same father, from whom the earth,
our nurturing mother, receives drops of liquid water.

The University of Bologna (founded in 1088) was the first university to be called an **alma mater**, when it adopted the motto **Alma mater studiorum** (**Nurturing mother of studies**).

Indirect Commands; Fear Clauses

Exercises

A. Translate each clause and state whether it is an indirect command or a clause of fearing. Also state whether it is in primary or secondary sequence and whether it describes an action that is occurring at the same time or time after the main verb, or whether it describes an action that has already been completed before the main verb.

1. Cives timent ne bellum civile mox incipiat.

2. Filia patri persuasit ut libertatem ancillae daret.

3. Puer timet ut pecunia inventa sit.

4. Puer timebat ut pecunia inventa esset.

5. Dux captivo imperavit ut in carcerem rediret.

6. Ab coquo petivimus ut cenam pararet.

7. Veremur ne via sit periculosa.

8. Coquus metuit ut satis cibi paravisset.

9. Nauta Caesarem monuit ne hieme navigaret.

10. Caesar Allobrogibus imperavit ut Helvetiis frumenti copiam darent.

B. Translate each of the following sentences and identify the type of clause (purpose, result, indirect command, or fear), whether it is in primary or secondary sequence, and whether it describes an action that is occurring at the same time or time after the main verb, or whether it describes an action that has already been completed before the main verb.

1. Cicero suo fratri persuadet ne ad bellum eat.

2. Cum militibus ad urbem currimus ut eam servemus.

3. Orator locutus est tamdiu ut fessi fieremus.

4. Timeo ne hostes nostram urbem vincant.

5. Meam sororem rogo ut Ciceronem in foro loquentem audiat.

6. Frater meus ad oppidum ambulavit ut magnum leonem videret.

7. Dominus servis imperat ut novum aedificium construant.

8. Vereor ut puella me amet.

9. Galli tam fortiter pugnaverunt ut Caesar non eos vinceret.

10. Populi in foro steterunt ut Ciceronem audirent.

C. Translate each sentence into Latin and state whether it is a purpose clause, result clause, fearing clause, or an indirect command.

1. Caesar commands his soldiers to build a bridge.

2. The soldiers feared that the bridge might be broken.

3. The soldiers worked so long that they built a good bridge.

4. Caesar waged war in order to expand the Roman empire.

5. I called my sister so many times that she became angry.

11

Cum Clauses

1. **Cum: Preposition vs. Subordinating Conjunction.** There are two different words in Latin that are both spelled **cum**. One word is a preposition that takes the ablative case and is usually translated as "with" or "by." The other word is a subordinating conjunction, and **the subordinating conjunction is the topic of this chapter.**

2. **A conjunction is a word that "conjoins" or joins together two clauses.** Words like "and," "but," "or," "if," and "when" are conjunctions. **A *subordinating* conjunction is a conjunction that joins a *subordinate* (or dependent) clause onto a main (or independent) clause.** Words like "if," "when," "since," and "although" are subordinating conjunctions. (A word such as "or," "and," or "but" that joins two independent clauses is called a "coordinating conjunction.")

3a. **In Latin, cum is a subordinating conjunction,** and it introduces two main types of subordinate clauses:

3b. **A cum-temporal clause tells when the action of the main clause occurred.** In a cum-temporal clause, cum is translated as "when," and it takes the indicative mood. These are very easy to translate and they will never cause you any trouble.

Examples:
Cum erat meridies, puer rediit domum.   When it was noon, the boy returned home.
Cum erat prima lux, dux signum dedit.   When it was dawn, the leader gave the signal.

In both of these examples, the **cum-temporal clause simply tells when the action of the main clause occurred**, and it takes the indicative.

3c. A cum-circumstantial clause tells the circumstances under which the action of the main clause occurs. In a cum-circumstantial clause, **cum** is translated as "when," "since," or "although," and it takes the subjunctive.

Examples in English:
When I was running to the store, I slipped on a banana peel.
Since I was late, I forgot to take my phone.
Although I was late, I took the time to feed my cat.

4a. There are three main subtypes of cum-circumstantial clauses in Latin, as illustrated by the three examples above.

4b. A cum-circumstantial *temporal* clause is translated as "when," but it describes the circumstances under which something occurred, not the time. In the first example above, the clause, "when I was running to the store" describes the circumstances under which the speaker slipped on the banana peel, not the time when it occurred.

4c. A cum-circumstantial *causal* clause is translated with "since," and it describes the **reason why** the action of the main clause occurred.

4d. A cum-circumstantial *concessive* clause is translated with "although," and it describes the circumstances **despite which** the action occurred. Sometimes a word such as **tamen** (nevertheless) in the main clause will signal that the cum-circumstantial clause is concessive.

Examples of cum-circumstantial clauses in Latin:

Cum viri venirent Romam, viderunt Forum.	When the men went to Rome, they saw the Forum.
Cum viri venirent Romam, potuerunt videre Forum.	Since the men went to Rome, they were able to see the Forum.
Cum viri venirent Romam, tamen non viderunt Forum.	Although the men went to Rome, they not see the Forum.

Nota bene (Note well): Sometimes a cum-circumstantial clause can be translated in more than one way. In these cases, you should look to the context to help you figure out how to translate it. The first example above could be translated with "since" and the second example could be translated with "when." The larger context of the sentence will help you decide the best way to translate it.

5. The tense of the subjunctive in a cum-circumstantial clause is determined by the sequence of tenses. All three examples above have an imperfect subjunctive showing same time in secondary sequence.

Cum Clauses

6. **Flow chart for cum:** When you see the word **cum** in a sentence, you can figure out how to translate it by using the following chart:

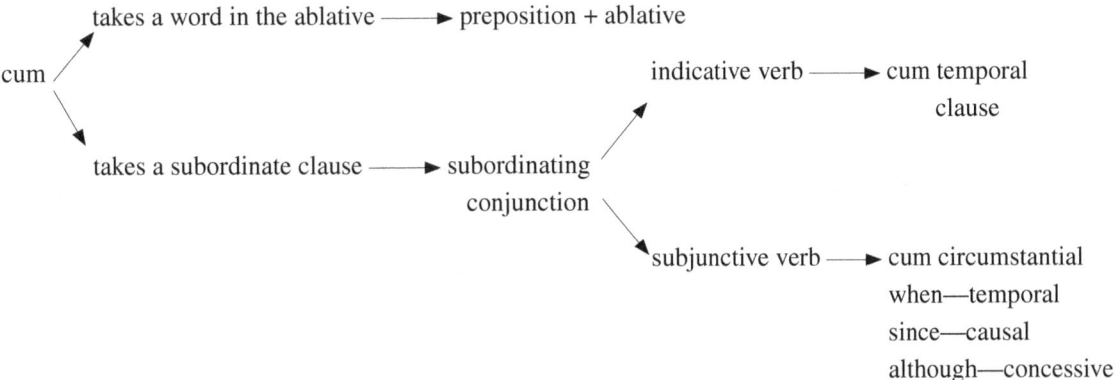

Lingua Latina Ubique

Here are some Latin legal terms.

Habeas corpus - You may have the body. This is a written order, issued by a judge, that requires someone who holds another person in custody to bring that person before the court. It is usually used on behalf of someone in police custody, requiring the police to either charge the arrested person with an offense or release that person.

Note that this phrase is a jussive subjunctive (the second person singular, present active subjunctive of **habeo, habere** and the accusative of **corpus**).

Alibi - Elsewhere. This word is a Latin adverb, meaning **elsewhere**, but it is used as a noun in English, referring to a claim or evidence that a person was elsewhere when a crime was committed, and therefore could not possibly have committed it.

Subpoena - Under penalty. This English noun is from the Latin phrase, **sub poena - under penalty,** and it refers to a written order issued by a court or other government agency, ordering a person to appear before that court or government agency by a specified date, or face a penalty for failure to do so.

Exercises

A. **Translate each of the following sentences and state whether the cum-clause is a cum-temporal or a cum-circumstantial clause. If it is a cum-circumstantial clause, state what sub-type it is.**

1. Cum vesper erat, sol occidit.

2. Cum pax in urbe esset, populus gaudebat.

3. Cum canis mortuus esset, puella dolebat.

4. Agricola aravit agros cum ver erat.

5. Cum pueri ab magistro laudarentur, tamen non erant felices.

6. Cum urbs deleta esset, populus fugit.

7. Cum multi gladiatores in arena moriantur, tamen pauci vivunt.

8. Cum tempestas Caesaris classem delevisset, nautae navigare ad Galliam non potuerunt.

9. Cum puer pulcherrimam urbem videret, stupuit.

10. Erat Aprilis cum Cicero ad vicinum oppidum iter fecit.

B. Translate the following sentences and identify the type of subordinate clause in each one: purpose, result, fear, indirect command, cum-temporal, or cum-circumstantial.

1. Cum infans militem videret, territus est.

2. Cum pater necatus esset, filius doluit.

3. Feci iter Athenas ut philosophiae studerem.

4. Cum defessus esset, tamen meus frater ad forum ambulavit.

5. Timeo ne hostes veniant.

6. Canis Caesaris tam sonore latravit ut Cicero moleste ferret.

7. Caesar imperavit militibus ne necarent feminas.

8. Cum Hercules esset fortis, non felix erat.

9. Cum prima lux erat, mare videbamus.

10. Cum videas araneam, times?

Cum Clauses

C. Translate the following English sentences into Latin and explain the grammar and syntax of each one.

1. Although I had lost the book, my father was not angry.

2. Mother ordered the maid to prepare the dinner.

3. When Remus had jumped over the wall, Romulus killed him.

4. The girl sang so sweetly that everyone wept.

5. Hercules killed the lion so that the people would be safe.

12

Conditions

1. **Conditional sentences are made up of two clauses:** an "if" clause (called the protasis) and a "then" clause, (called the apodosis). The protasis is the subordinate (or dependent) clause while the apodosis is the main (or independent) clause.

   Example: "If you are reading this, then you are studying Latin."

2. The word **protasis** is from the Greek προτείνω (proteinō), meaning "stretch before," and logically it forms the premise, which is metaphorically "stretched before" or proposed to the reader. The word **apodosis** is from the Greek ἀποδίδωμι (apodidōmi), meaning "give back," and logically it forms the conclusion, which is metaphorically "given back" to the proposer.

3. **In Latin, there are six types of conditions,** and they are listed below in a descending order of reality (or vividness). The first three types of conditions use the indicative mood (above the gray bar) and the last three types (below the gray bar) use the subjunctive.

4a. Six Types of Conditions

1.	simple present	present indicative in both clauses
2.	simple past	past indicative in both clauses
3.	future more vivid	future indicative in both clauses
4.	future less vivid	present subjunctive in both clauses
5.	present contrary to fact	imperfect subjunctive in both clauses
6.	past contrary to fact	pluperfect subjunctive in both clauses

4b. In a **future more vivid condition**, the Romans would sometimes use a **future perfect** in the **protasis** (instead of a future indicative), but this is usually not reflected in the English translation.

5. **Examples in English: Simple Conditions** are just like conditions in English, and you can translate them naturally; they will never give you any trouble.

    In English, Future More Vivid Conditions usually have their protasis in the present tense and their apodosis in the future: "If we get up early tomorrow, we will see the sunrise." In this sentence, the protasis is expressed in the present tense (for greater vividness) even though it is understood to describe a future event.

    In English, Future Less Vivid Conditions are usually expressed with the formula should/would: "If we should see a whale tomorrow, we would be lucky." For this reason, future less vivid conditions are sometimes referred to as "should/would conditions." They describe an event that may or may not occur in the future.

    Contrary-to-Fact Conditions are rarely used in English, which is why they seem more difficult to us. But once you have practiced with some examples in English, they will become easier.

    Present Contrary-to-Fact Conditions:
    If I were in Greece right now, I would be lying on the beach. (But I am not in Greece right now, so I am not lying on the beach.)
    If I were clairvoyant, I could see the future. (But I am not clairvoyant, so I cannot see the future.)
    If that man were taller, he would be able to play basketball. (But he is not taller, so he is not able to play basketball.)
    Can you think of some more examples?

    Past Contrary-to-Fact Conditions:
    If I had eaten breakfast this morning, I would not have been hungry during class. (But I did not eat breakfast this morning, so I was hungry during class.)
    If I had taken more math classes in high school, I would have been able to calculate that percentage. (But I did not take more math classes in high school, so I was not able to calculate that percentage.)
    If she had not forgotten her cellphone, we could have called for help. (But she did forget her cellphone, so we could not call for help.)
    Can you think of some more examples?

6. In Latin, the protasis of a condition is usually introduced by **si** (if) or **nisi** (if not, unless).

7. Examples in Latin:

1.	simple present—pres indic	Si puer veritatem dicit, sapiens est. If the boy speaks the truth, he is wise.
2.	simple past—past indic	Si puer veritatem dixit, sapiens erat. If the boy spoke the truth, he was wise.
3.	future more vivid—fut indic	Si puer veritatem dicet, sapiens erit. If the boy speaks the truth, he will be wise.
4.	future less vivid—pres subj	Si puer veritatem dicat, sapiens sit. If the boy should speak the truth, he would be wise.
5.	present contrary to fact—imperf subj	Si puer veritatem diceret, sapiens esset. If the boy were speaking the truth, he would be wise. (But he isn't.)
6.	past contrary to fact—pluperf subj	Si puer veritatem dixisset, sapiens fuisset. If the boy had spoken the truth, he would have been wise. (But he wasn't.)

Lingua Latina Ubique

Some brand names taken from (or similar to) Latin words. Can you think of any others?

Pergo - I go forward. This flooring company is especially known for making laminate floors that look like wood but are much more durable.

Volvo - I roll. The well-known Swedish car company.

Prius - Prior, superior, preferable, better. This hybrid gas-electric car manufactured by Toyota was first produced in 1997.

Altima - Highest, most elevated, most lofty. This mid-size sedan has been manufactured by Nissan since 1992.

Optima - Best, most worthy, most choiceworthy. This mid-size sedan was manufactured by Kia from 2000 to 2021.

Formica: This hard, heat-resistant surface commonly used for countertops has the same name as the Latin word for **ant**. The company claims, however, that it was not named after the hard exoskeleton of that animal, but rather from the fact that Formica was originally used to replace the mineral mica in electrical applications, and thus the name "for mica."

CONDITIONS

Vespa: This is a brand of scooter produced by the Italian company Piaggio since 1946. It means **wasp** in both Latin and Italian. The name comes from the shape of the scooter: The larger front and rear are connected by a narrow waist, and the handles look like antennae. But the scooter was given this name because **vespa** is the word for **wasp** in Italian; it just happens to be the same word in Latin.

Exercises

A. Translate each of the following sentences and label the type of condition it is.

1. Si magister fabulam narrat, eam audimus.

2. Si latro gemmam reddisset, mater laeta fuisset.

3. Si faciat iter Romam, forum videat.

4. Si servi agros araverunt, negotium perfecerunt.

5. Si Lesbia Catullum amaret, eum basiaret.

6. Si serpentem videbimus, eum necabimus.

7. Si serpentem vidissemus, eum necavissemus.

8. Si amicus meus es, felix sum.

9. Si urbs deleatur, populus fugiat.

10. Si magister discipulum laudavisset, felicior fuisset.

B. Translate each of the following sentences, and label the use of the subjunctive in each one.

1. Utinam domi mansissemus!

2. Narremne malum nuntium aut taceam?

3. Nostri milites tam fortiter pugnaverunt ut urbem hostium delerent.

4. Servus in oppidum ambulavit ut cibum emeret.

5. Si Cicero orationem habuisset, omnes audivissent.

6. Cum Catullus non opulentus esset, sacculus eius vacuus erat.

7. Cum Catullus non opulentus esset, tamen felix erat.

8. Si senator esses, meliores leges scibere posses.

9. Dux nos monuit ne istam urbem opulentam oppugnaremus.

10. Cicero timet ne bellum civile Romam deleat.

C. Translate the following English sentences into Latin and explain the syntax of each.

1. The danger was so great that the citizens departed from the city.

2. The citizens departed from the city in order to escape from great danger.

3. Since the danger was so great, the soldiers saved the people.

4. If the soldiers had come sooner, they would have saved the people.

5. The citizens feared that the soldiers would not save the city.

13

Relative Clauses

Forms

1. **In both English and Latin, a relative pronoun** (such as "who," "which," or "that") **relates two clauses by making one clause subordinate to the other**.

    For example, two sentences ("I love the girl." "The girl is wearing a red dress.") can be placed in relationship to one another with the relative pronoun **who**: "I love the girl who is wearing a red dress."

    In this example, the relative pronoun "who" **relates** the two clauses by making the relative clause ("who is wearing a red dress") subordinate to the main clause ("I love the girl").

    Therefore, in both English and Latin, **a relative clause is a subordinate clause that is attached to the main clause by a relative pronoun.**

    In both English and Latin, a relative pronoun always has an antecedent, the word or phrase (usually in the previous clause) to which the relative pronoun refers. In the example, "I love the girl who is wearing a red dress," the antecedent of the relative pronoun "who" is "the girl."

2. In Latin, the relative pronoun is **qui, quae, quod** ("who" or "which"). Please review the declension of the relative pronoun and make sure you know all of its forms.

Sing | | | | Plu
	M	F	N		M	F	N
nom	quī	quae	quod		quī	quae	quae
gen	cūius	cūius	cūius		quōrum	quārum	quōrum
dat	cui	cui	cui		quibus	quibus	quibus
acc	quem	quam	quod		quōs	quās	quae
abl	quō	quā	quō		quibus	quibus	quibus

Chapter 13

Nota bene: In English, the relative pronoun **who** has kept its declension. Please review the following table and make sure you can use the English relative pronoun correctly.

nom (subject)	who
gen (possession)	whose
dat (ind. object)	to whom, for whom
acc (dir. object)	whom
abl (instrumental)	by whom, with whom

3. Memorize this rule: **In Latin, the gender and number of a relative pronoun is determined by its antecedent, but its case is determined by its function in its own clause.**

4. **Relative pronouns are rapidly disappearing in English usage,** which makes them seem more difficult in Latin than they really are. For this reason, we have added an exercise on relative pronouns in English to make you more comfortable with using them in Latin. Please do this exercise now, before continuing with the rest of this chapter.

Exercise on Relative Pronouns in English

Fill in the blanks: In Latin, a relative pronoun takes its _____ and _____ from its antecedent, but it takes its _____ from its function in _____.

In the sentences below, circle the relative pronoun, underline its antecedent and draw an arrow from the relative pronoun to its antecedent. Then draw a box around the relative clause. Finally, state what the case and number of the relative pronoun would be if it were in Latin.

1. The Cyclops was a huge monster who had only one eye, which was in the center of his head.

2. The Cyclops, whose name was Polyphemus, lived on an island, which I have never seen.

3. Polyphemus had many sheep and goats who gave him milk, from which he made cheese, which he greatly enjoyed.

4. Odysseus, whose home was in Ithaca, was a sailor who was very curious about the people whom he met.

5. Odysseus had twelve men whom he called his companions, whose names I don't know.

6. Odysseus ate some cheeses, the owner of which was Polyphemus, the Cyclops whom I previously mentioned.

7. Polyphemus returned to the cave, which he had left that morning, and rolled a huge rock, which was lying nearby, in front of the opening, which was the only entrance to the cave.

8. Now Odysseus and his men were trapped, a fact which troubled them greatly.

9. Odysseus gave Polyphemus some wine, which he had brought with him.

10. Odysseus, whose cleverness was well known, told Polyphemus that his name was "No Man," which was a lie.

11. The Cyclops enjoyed the wine which Odysseus had brought, which soon made him drunk.

12. Odysseus saw a tall tree trunk, which was lying on the floor of the cave, the end of which he sharpened.

13. They put the pointed end of the pole which they had made into the fire, which was burning.

14. They stabbed the Cyclops, who was snoring loudly, in the eye with the pole, which was now very hot.

15. Polyphemus, whose screams were deafening, could not catch Odysseus and his men, whom he could no longer see.

16. Polyphemus's neighbors, who heard the screams, asked Polyphemus who was hurting him.

17. Polyphemus, who was not very bright, said that "No Man" was hurting him, an answer which he thought was correct.

18. This story is told in the *Odyssey*, which was composed by Homer, whose identity may never be known.

Usage

5. **Relative Clauses of Fact: In Latin, relative clauses that state a fact about the antecedent take the indicative mood.** You can translate them naturally, and they will never cause you any trouble. Note that **Relative Clauses of Fact** can be false; that is, they can state a fact that happens not to be true.

6. **Relative Clauses of Characteristic and Purpose:** There are several types of relative clauses in Latin that take the subjunctive. In all types, the tense of the subjunctive follows the sequence of tenses. We will discuss only the two most common types here: **Relative Clauses of Characteristic** and **Relative Clauses of Purpose**.

7. **Relative Clauses of Characteristic state a characteristic of the antecedent**, not a fact. **The verb is in the subjunctive.** Consider the following examples.

Caesar non est qui hoc fecit.	Fact: Caesar is not the person who did this.
Caesar non est qui hoc faciat.	Characteristic: Caesar is not the sort of person who would do this.
Hic est liber quem omnes legunt.	Fact: This is the book which everyone is reading.
Hic est liber quem omnes legant.	Characteristic: This is the sort of book which everyone reads.

8. **In the above examples, the only way to recognize a relative clause of characteristic is that the verb is in the subjunctive.** Sometimes, however, a relative clause of characteristic will have a general antecedent, such as **sunt qui** (there are those who), or **nemo est qui** (there is no one who), etc.

    Examples:
Nemo erat qui hoc faceret.	There was no one [of the sort] who would do this.
Sunt qui mortem timeant.	There are those [of the sort] who fear death.

    In both of these examples, the relative clause does not state a fact, but rather it describes a sort of person who would (or would not) characteristically act in a certain way.

9. **Relative Clauses of Purpose:** A relative clause of purpose uses a relative pronoun (**qui, quae, quod**) or a relative adverb (**ubi, unde, quo**) to introduce a purpose clause. Although **ut** or **ne + subjunctive** was the most common way to introduce a purpose clause in Latin, the Romans had many other ways to indicate purpose, one of which was the **relative clause of purpose**. A relative clause of purpose takes the subjunctive.

    Examples:
Caesar legatos misit, qui dicerent nuntium.	Caesar sent envoys so that they would tell the news. (Or: Caesar sent envoys to tell the news.)
Cicero puero librum dedit quem legeret.	Cicero gave the boy a book in order that he might read it. (Or: Cicero gave the boy a book so that he might read it.)
Non habebant locum quo se reciperent.	They did not have a place to which they might flee. (i.e., for the purpose of refuge.)

Nota Bene: As you can see from these examples, the relative clause of purpose is very similar to the relative clause of characteristic and may even have developed from it. Nonetheless, it is intended to show purpose, and it should be translated as such wherever possible.

Also note that the relative clause of purpose can be translated in several different ways.

Nota Bene: The relative clause of purpose is frequently used after the verb **mitto**, as in the first example above.

10. **Relative Clause of Purpose with a comparative:** Latin frequently uses a relative clause of purpose with **quo** in combination with a comparative adjective or adverb. In these clauses, **quo** can be translated literally as "by which the + comparative."

    Study the following examples.
    Lupus iussit puellam propinquare quo eam melius videret. The wolf ordered the girl to approach, in order that he might see her better. Lit: "by which the better he might see her."
    Dux usus est raedā quo facilius iter faceret. The commander used a carriage in order that he might make the journey more easily. Lit: "by which the more easily he might make the journey."

11. The Romans sometimes used a **neuter relative pronoun (singular or plural) at the beginning of a sentence to refer back to an object or idea in the previous sentence**. In most cases, the best way to translate these into English is to use a **demonstrative pronoun**, rather than a relative pronoun. Here are some examples.

quae cum ita sint	**literal translation:**	since which things are so
	smoother translation:	since these things are so
quo factum est	**literal translation:**	by which it happened
	smoother translation:	by this it happened
quibus rebus cognitis	**literal translation:**	with which things having become known
	smoother translation:	with these things having become known
	even smoother:	when these things were known

Lingua Latina Ubique

e.g. (exempli gratiā) - For the sake of an example or simply, **for example.**
Note that **gratiā,** in the ablative, is a preposition meaning **for the sake of,** and takes a preceding genitive.
Do not confuse with **i.e. (id est - that is, in other words**), discussed in Chapter 9. The abbreviation **i.e.** signals that the following words will repeat what the author is trying to say in different (often simpler) terms, while **e.g.** signals that the following words will be **examples** of what was previously said.

Ipso facto - By the fact itself, or **by this very fact.** This term is used to indicate that one situation is the logical or natural consequence of another.

Example: "Because he was born in the United States, he is, *ipso facto*, an American citizen."

Note that this is an expression in the ablative (used as an ablative of means) combining the ablative of **factum** (a neuter noun meaning **fact, deed,** or **act**) with the ablative of the intensive adjective **ipse, ipsa, ipsum - himself, herself, itself.**

Quid pro quo - Something for something. This Latin phrase seems to have originated in the 1560s with the meaning of substituting one ingredient for another in a recipe. For example: "You can use honey instead of sugar in this recipe, as a *quid pro quo*."

Today, however, the phrase usually refers to an illicit or unethical (and often unspoken) agreement, in which one person receives a favor but is expected to do a favor for the giver in return.

Example: "He took me out to dinner, but later that evening he expected a *quid pro quo*."

The Latin word **quis** (M&F), **quid** (N) can be an indefinite pronoun meaning **something** or **anything**, as it is here. (The word can also be used as an interrogative pronoun, meaning **who?, which?,** or **what?**.) Its use as an indefinite pronoun may have originated as a shortened form of **aliquis, aliquid - anyone/someone** and **anything/something**.

Exercises

A. Translate each of the following relative clauses, and state whether it is a relative clause of fact, characteristic, or purpose.

1. Imperator multos milites misit qui hostes interficerent.

2. Mater epistulam quam filius postea lēgit scripsit.

3. Est nihil quod illi fortes milites vereatur sed dedecus.

4. Odysseus montem ascendit quo clarius insulam videret.

5. Rex milites ad urbem duxit qui liberos servarent.

6. Sunt aliqui oratores qui populo persuadeant.

7. Magister cui veritas dicta est veniam puero dedit.

8. Poeta poemata scripsit quo melius magnitudinem animi exprimeret.

9. Non est ullus discipulus qui magistrum non timeat.

10. Epistula quam teneo longa est.

B. Translate the following sentences and identify the use of the subjunctive where appropriate.

1. Puella laboravit ut pecuniam obtineret.

2. Mater filium totiens vocavit ut irasceretur.

3. Cum Eurydice serpentem vidit, pertimuit.

4. Cum Eurydice pertimesceret, non clamavit.

5. Orpheus non erat qui fato facile cederet.

6. Lyra Orphei cecinit tam dulciter ut Pluto fleret.

7. Si Orpheus non respexisset, Eurydice non mortua esset.

8. Imperator laudavit milites quo acrius urbem hostium impugnarent.

9. Timeo ne milites nostram urbem impugnent.

10. Imperator milites misit qui explorarent castra hostium.

C. Translate the following English sentences into Latin and explain the syntax of each one.

1. Cicero gave an oration in the Senate in which he criticized Catiline.

2. Catiline was not the sort of person who would feel shame. (Use a relative clause of characteristic.)

3. Although Catiline fought bravely, nevertheless he was killed.

4. Caesar sent envoys to announce his plans to the Helvetii. (Use a relative clause of purpose.)

5. Caesar set out for the land beyond the Po River so that he might spend the winter more pleasantly. (Use a relative clause of purpose.)

14

Indirect Questions

1. **Indirect questions are reported questions.** Consider the following examples.

Where did you go?	Direct Question
I wonder where you went.	Indirect Question
I know where you went.	Indirect Question
Twinkle, twinkle, little star, what are you?	Direct Question
Twinkle, twinkle, little star, how I wonder what you are.	Indirect Question
Scientists can now explain what stars are and how they are formed.	Indirect Question
What did you do last summer?	Direct Question.
I asked your mother what you did last summer.	Indirect Question
Your mother told me what you did last summer.	Indirect Question
I know what you did last summer.	Indirect Question
Who let the dogs out?	Direct Question
I wonder who let the dogs out.	Indirect Question
My sister knows who let the dogs out.	Indirect Question

   Nota Bene: As the above examples show, indirect questions are introduced by a word of asking, wondering, knowing, telling, hearing, etc., followed by a question word (where, what, how, when, etc.) and then a question. **Indirect questions are followed by a period, not a question mark, because they are actually statements about a question; they are not questions themselves.**

2. In English, the word order of a direct question is often reversed in an indirect question. **In Latin, the word order does not change, but the mood of the verb is changed to the subjunctive. The tense of the subjunctive follows the sequence of tenses.**

Examples:
Quid Cicero dixit? — What did Cicero say? Direct Question
Catilina miratur quid Cicero dicat. — Catiline wonders what Cicero is saying. Indirect Question
Catilina audivit quid Cicero diceret. — Catiline heard what Cicero was saying. Indirect Question
Catilina audivit quid Cicero dixisset. — Catiline heard what Cicero had said. Indirect Question

Nota Bene: A sentence in which one person asks another person to do something is an indirect command (not an indirect question), even if a question word is used. Examples:

Cicero rogavit Catilinam ut discederet ex urbe. (Indirect Command)
Cicero asked Catiline to leave the city. (Literally: Cicero asked Catiline that he leave from the city.)

Cicero rogavit Catilinam quid vellet. (Indirect Question)
Cicero asked Catiline what he wanted.

Lingua Latina Ubique

Persona non grata - Person not welcome. This phrase is used in diplomacy to refer to a person who is not welcome in a particular country. After being declared **persona non grata**, a person must leave the country immediately (or may be denied entrance).

Example: "After his son's traffic accident, the diplomat was declared *persona non grata* and he and his family were forced to leave the country."

The phrase is also used in a more informal sense to refer to someone who is not welcome to others. For example: "After I asked him about his divorce, I became *persona non grata*."

Prima facie: Literally **at first face** or **at first appearance**, this phrase is used with the meaning **at first sight** or **based on first impression.**

As a legal term, it generally means that something seems to be true on first appearance, but is subject to further evidence or proof.

Example: "When I saw my husband in a bar with my best friend, on *prima facie* evidence, I thought they were having an affair. But later he explained that he was only helping her with her income taxes."

Veto - I forbid. In English, this word is used as a verb ("He vetoed the bill."), as an adjective ("The governor has veto power over this legislation."), and as a noun ("I worry about the president's veto.") to refer to an official's power to prevent a proposed bill from becoming a law.

In ancient Rome, this was the word by which the tribunes of the people could declare their objection to any measure proposed by the Senate or the magistrates, thus preventing it from being enacted.

Indirect Questions

Bona fides - Good faith. This Latin phrase is pronounced (even in English) with a classical Latin pronunciation (**bona fi-des**) and is used to mean the experience or credentials that establish a person's reputation in a particular area of expertise.
  Examples:
  He used his successful run for the senate to establish his political bona fides.
  After her successful cooking show, no one questioned her culinary bona fides.

Bona fide. The same Latin phrase in the ablative case is used in English as an adjective meaning real or genuine. In this usage, the phrase is given an English pronunciation (with **fide** pronounced as a single syllable).
  Example: This is a bona fide moon rock; it is made of armalcolite.

Exercises

A. Translate the following indirect questions, paying careful attention to the sequence of tenses.

1. Puella scit quis ad cenam veniat.

2. Puella scivit quis ad cenam veniret.

3. Puella scit quis ad cenam venerit.

4. Puella scivit quis ad cenam venisset.

5. Nescio ubi mater sit.

6. Nescio ubi mater fuerit.

7. Nescivi ubi mater esset.

8. Nescivi ubi mater fuisset.

9. Pater rogat cur fur pecuniam reddeat.

10. Pater rogavit cur fur pecuniam redderet.

11. Pater rogavit cur fur pecuniam reddidisset.

12. Pater rogat cur fur pecuniam reddiderit.

13. Caesar rogat si oraculum consultum sit.

14. Senex scit ubi thesaurus sit.

15. Miror si discipuli defessi sint.

B. Translate the following sentences and explain the use of the subjunctive in each one.

1. Graeci equum ligneum aedificaverunt ut Troiam caperent.

2. Cum Troiani equum ligneum in urbem portavissent, Graeci Troiam ceperunt.

3. Aeneas rogavit Anchisen ut urbe excederet.

4. Anchises scit cur astrum ceciderit ex caelo.

5. Creusa timebat ne viam suam perderet.

6. Si dii favissent Troiam, Graeci non eam delēre potuissent.

7. Aeneas misit sodales qui bonum locum ad urbem condendam invenirent.

8. Aeneas rogat Sibyllam quomodo profisceretur ad inferos.

9. Aeneas vult venire ad inferos ut videat manes patris Anchisae.

10. Dido rogavit utrum Aeneas pius esset.

C. Translate the following English sentences into Latin and explain the syntax of each one.

1. The people asked the king if the omen was good.

2. The commander ordered his soldiers to prepare the camp.

3. Aeneas wonders whether he should speak or keep silent.

4. Turnus asks Latinus where his (Turnus's) bride is.

5. Venus begs Cupid to shoot an arrow.

15

Subordinate Clauses in Indirect Discourse; Subjunctive of a Reported Reason

Subordinate Clauses in Indirect Discourse

1. As discussed in Chapter 5, indirect statement (or discourse) in Latin takes the accusative/infinitive construction. Sometimes, however, indirect discourse includes one or more subordinate clauses. **Subordinate clauses in indirect discourse are not put into accusative/ infinitive construction, but their verbs are put into the subjunctive.**

   Examples:
   Pompeius vidit canem quem Caesar possidet. Pompey sees the dog which Caesar owns.
   Scio Pompeium videre canem quem Caesar possideat. I know that Pompey sees the dog which Caesar owns.

   Milites qui in castris manent sunt fortes. The soldiers who remain in camp are brave.
   Imperator dixit milites qui in castris manerent esse fortes. The general said that the soldiers who remained in the camp were brave.

   Nota Bene: The tense of the subjunctive in the subordinate clause follows the sequence of tenses. Also, remember that the tense of the infinitive in indirect discourse is relative to the tense of the introductory verb (see Chapter 5, section 13).

   Si puer linguam Latinam discit, est sapiens. If the boy learns Latin, he is wise.
   Pater dicit si puer linguam Latinam discat, esse sapientem. Father says that if the boy is learning Latin, he is wise.
   Pater dixit si puer linguam Latinam disceret, esse sapientem. Father said that if the boy was learning Latin, he was wise.

   Nota Bene: Remember that in a condition, the protasis (if-clause) is a subordinate clause, while the apodosis (then-clause) is an independent clause.

91

CHAPTER 15

Subjunctive of a Reported Reason

2. The words **quod**, **quia**, and **quoniam**, which all mean "because," can introduce causal clauses. (As we learned in Chapter 11, **cum** can also introduce a clausal clause.) All causal clauses are subordinate clauses.

3. **Quod, quia,** and **quoniam** take the **indicative** when the reason given is that of the writer or speaker; they take the **subjunctive when the reason is that of another person**. This is a subtle difference in grammar, but it can have a big difference in meaning, so make sure to notice in every causal clause whether the verb is in the indicative or subjunctive mood.

Examples:
Imperator socios flumen transire noluit quod non eis confidebat. The general did not allow the allies to cross the river because he did not trust them. (The writer is giving his own explanation.)
Imperator socios flumen transire noluit quod non eis confideret. The general did not allow the allies to cross the river because (as he said), he did not trust them. (The writer is reporting the general's explanation, which the writer may or may not agree with.)

Servus punitus est quod argentum furatus erat. The slave was punished because he had stolen the silver. (The writer agrees with the reason and states it as a fact.)
Servus punitus est quod argentum furatus esset. The slave was punished because he allegedly had stolen the silver. (The writer explains that this was the reason given for the punishment, but does not necessarily endorse it.)

Socrates accusatus est quod iuventutem corrumpebat. Socrates was indicted because he was corrupting the youth. (The writer agrees with the reason given.)
Socrates accusatus est quod iuventutem corrumperet. Socrates was indicted on the grounds that he was corrupting the youth. (The writer does not necessarily agree with the reason that was given.)

Nota Bene: There is no single formula for translating the subjunctive of a reported reason; you should translate it according to the context.

Lingua Latina Ubique

Post hoc ergo propter hoc - After this therefore because of this. Post hoc ergo propter hoc is a logical fallacy in which one thing happens after another and the first event is (falsely) assumed to have caused the second event. This phrase is often simply called a **post hoc fallacy**.

An example of a **post hoc fallacy** would be "Last year I went to the Red Sox game wearing my favorite red shirt and the Red Sox won! Now I always wear that same red shirt when the Red Sox play; I think it helps."

A more dangerous example is the false association between childhood vaccinations and autism. Just because some children who are vaccinated later develop autism does not mean that the vaccines caused the autism.

Post hoc fallacy is a type of magical thinking (when two unrelated events are assumed to be closely connected), and (as Joan Didion famously showed in her 2005 book, *The Year of Magical Thinking*) it is something we are all capable of.

Citius, altius, fortius - Faster, higher, stronger. This is the official motto of the modern Olympic Games. It is meant to embody the ideal of striving for excellence that the Olympics are supposed to represent.

Note that this motto is made from the neuter comparative adjectives (which are also the comparative adverbs) of the adjectives **citus, -a, -um** - fast, quick, swift; **altus, -a, -um** - high, lofty, tall or deep, profound; and **fortis, forte** - strong, brave.

Ne plus ultra - Do not [go] beyond. According to a Renaissance tradition, this warning was supposedly inscribed on the Pillars of Hercules (on either side of the Straits of Gibraltar, between Spain and Morocco, which separate the Mediterranean Sea from the Atlantic Ocean), warning sailors not to travel beyond the edge of the known world.

If this story is true, an imperative for going or traveling (such as **ite,** the second person plural imperative of **eo**) was probably understood.

Whether this story is true or not, this expression is used today to describe the best or most excellent example of something; a thing that is so great that nothing could possibly surpass or outdo it.
Example: "The Maserati is the *ne plus ultra* of sports cars."

Exercises

A. Translate the following sentences and explain the syntax of each one.

1. Amulius iussit milites ponere fratrem Numitorem qui fuisset rex Albae Longae in carcerem.

2. Rhea Silvia, filia Numitoris, facta est sacerdos Vestae quia esset pura et sancta.

3. Quod Numitor in carcere erat, Amulius fiebat rex.

4. Rhea Silvia dixit patrem Romuli et Remi qui essent sui filii esse Martem.

5. Amulius posuit Romulum et Remum in Tiberem quod eos timuit.

6. Amulius posuit Romulum et Remum in Tiberem quod videret malum omen.

7. Romulus et Remus superfuerunt quia lupa eos nutrivisset.

8. Faustulus, pastor regius, dixit pueros qui essent fortes et pulchri esse suos filios.

9. Faustulus et uxor Larentia credebant pueros qui apud se educati essent nepotes Numitoris esse.

10. Romulus et Remus fecerunt impetum in latrones quod furati essent praedam.

11. Latrones irati quod praeda eorum amissa erat Remum ceperunt et duxerunt eum ad regem Amulium. Latrones dixit Remum qui esset filius pastoris esse latronem.

B. Translate the following sentences and explain the syntax of each one.

1. Numitor agnovit Remum qui iam fortis iuvenis esset suum nepotem esse.

2. Romulus et Remus cum manu pastorum tantum impetum in Amulium fecerunt ut rex interficeretur.

3. Cum Numitor regnum Albae Longae receperit, omnes gaudebant.

4. Iam Romulus et Remus nesciebant quid facerent. Constituerunt condere urbem quem ipsi regnare possent.

5. Quod uterque iuvenis suum nomen novae urbi dare cupivit, iudicium auguriis habuerunt.

6. Gemini fratres aspiciebant caelum ut spectarent omina.

7. Remus prius vīdit sex vultures sed quia Romulus postea duodecim videret gemini non convenire potuerunt.

8. Romulus muros urbis aedificabat cum Remus eos transiliret ut fratrem illuderet.

9. Romulus timebat ne Remus suam potestatem provocaret. Itaque Romulus strinxit gladium quo fratrem interficeret.

10. Romani mirantur quare urbs suacum violentia condita sit.

SUBORDINATE CLAUSES IN INDIRECT DISCOURSE; SUBJUNCTIVE OF A REPORTED REASON

C. Translate the following English sentences into Latin and explain the syntax of each one.

1. The commander ordered the soldiers to build a strong wall. (use **impero** + dat. pers.)

2. The mother looked for an omen which would foretell a good outcome.

3. The senate feared that a civil war would be waged.

4. Father used a sundial in order to know the time more easily. (use a relative clause of purpose)

5. If Dido had never seen Aeneas, she would have had a long life.

Grammatical Appendix

NOUNS

First Declension

Sing	puella, -ae, f - girl
nominative/vocative	puella
genitive	puellae
dative	puellae
accusative	puellam
ablative	puellā
Plu	
nominative/vocative	puellae
genitive	puellārum
dative	puellīs
accusative	puellās
ablative	puellīs

Second Declension

Sing	hortus, -ī, m - garden	bellum, -ī n - war	puer, -ī, m - boy	ager, -grī, m - field	vir, -ī m - man
nom	hortus	bellum	puer	ager	vir
gen	hortī	bellī	puerī	agrī	virī
dat	hortō	bellō	puerō	agrō	virō
acc	hortum	bellum	puerum	agrum	virum
abl	hortō	bellō	puerō	agrō	virō
voc	horte	bellum	puer	ager	vir
Plu					
nom/voc	hortī	bella	puerī	agrī	virī
gen	hortōrum	bellōrum	puerōrum	agrōrum	virōrum
dat	hortīs	bellīs	puerīs	agrīs	virīs
acc	hortōs	bella	puerōs	agrōs	virōs
abl	hortīs	bellīs	puerīs	agrīs	virīs

Third Declension—Consonant Stems

Sing	rēx, rēgis, m - king	corpus, corporis, n - body
nom/voc	rēx	corpus
gen	rēgis	corporis
dat	rēgī	corporī
acc	rēgem	corpus
abl	rēge	corpore
Plu		
nom/voc	rēgēs	corpora
gen	rēgum	corporum
dat	rēgibus	corporibus
acc	rēgēs	corpora
abl	rēgibus	corporibus

Third Declension - I-Stems

Sing	cīvis, -is, m - citizen	urbs, -is, f - city	mare, -is, n - sea
nom/voc	cīvis	urbs	mare
gen	cīvis	urbis	maris
dat	cīvī	urbī	marī
acc	cīvem	urbem	mare
abl	cīve	urbe	marī
Plu			
nom/voc	cīvēs	urbēs	maria
gen	cīvium	urbium	marium
dat	cīvibus	urbibus	maribus
acc	cīvēs or īs	urbēs or -īs	maria
abl	cīvibus	urbibus	maribus

Third Declension - Irregular

Sing	vīs, vīs, f - force
nom/voc	vīs
gen	(vīs)
dat	(vī)
acc	vim
abl	vī

Plu	
nom/voc	vīrēs
gen	vīrium
dat	vīribus
acc	vīrēs
abl	vīribus

Fourth Declension

Sing	frūctus, -ūs, m - fruit	cornū, -ūs, n - horn
nom/voc	frūctus	cornū
gen	frūctūs	cornūs
dat	frūctuī	cornū
acc	frūctum	cornū
abl	frūctū	cornū
Plu		
nom/voc	frūctūs	cornua
gen	frūctuum	cornuum
dat	frūctibus	cornibus
acc	frūctūs	cornua
abl	frūctibus	cornibus

Fifth Declension

Sing	diēs, diēī, m - day	rēs, reī, f - thing
nom/voc	diēs	rēs
gen	diēī	reī
dat	diēī	reī
acc	diem	rem
abl	diē	rē
Plu		
nom/voc	diēs	rēs
gen	diērum	rērum
dat	diēbus	rēbus
acc	diēs	rēs
abl	diēbus	rēbus

GRAMMATICAL APPENDIX

ADJECTIVES

FIRST AND SECOND DECLENSIONS

magnus, -a, um - large, great

	Masculine	Feminine	Neuter
Sing			
nom	magnus	magna	magnum
gen	magnī	magnae	magnī
dat	magnō	magnae	magnō
acc	magnum	magnam	magnum
abl	magnō	magnā	magnō
voc	magne	magna	magnum
Plu			
nom/voc	magnī	magnae	magna
gen	magnōrum	magnārum	magnōrum
dat	magnīs	magnīs	magnīs
acc	magnōs	magnās	magna
abl	magnīs	magnīs	magnīs

līber, lībera, līberum - free

	Masculine	Feminine	Neuter
Sing			
nom/voc	līber	lībera	līberum
gen	līberī	līberae	līberī
dat	līberō	līberae	līberō
acc	līberum	līberam	līberum
abl	līberō	līberā	līberō
Plu			
nom/voc	līberī	līberae	lībera
gen	līberōrum	līberārum	līberōrum
dat	līberīs	līberīs	līberīs
acc	līberōs	līberās	lībera
abl	līberīs	līberīs	līberīs

sacer, sacra, sacrum - sacred

	Masculine	Feminine	Neuter
Sing			
nom/voc	sacer	sacra	sacrum
gen	sacrī	sacrae	sacrī
dat	sacrō	sacrae	sacrō
acc	sacrum	sacram	sacrum
abl	sacrō	sacrā	sacrō
Plu			
nom/voc	sacrī	sacrae	sacra
gen	sacrōrum	sacrārum	sacrōrum
dat	sacrīs	sacrīs	sacrīs
acc	sacrōs	sacrās	sacra
abl	sacrīs	sacrīs	sacrīs

IRREGULAR FIRST AND SECOND DECLENSIONS

sōlus, -a, -um - alone, only

	Masculine	Feminine	Neuter
Sing			
nom	sōlus	sōla	sōlum
gen	sōlīus	sōlīus	sōlīus
dat	sōlī	sōlī	sōlī
acc	sōlum	sōlam	sōlum
abl	sōlō	sōlā	sōlō
Plu			
nom	sōlī	sōlae	sōla
gen	sōlōrum	sōlārum	sōlōrum
dat	sōlīs	sōlīs	sōlīs
acc	sōlōs	sōlās	sōla
abl	sōlīs	sōlīs	sōlīs

Similarly declined are the following irregular adjectives:
ūnus, unīus - one
tōtus, tōtīus - whole
alter, -era, -erum, alterīus - the other (of two)
ūllus, ūllīus - any
nūllus, nūllīus - none, no
alius, alterīus - another

Third Declension

	Two Endings		Three Endings		One Ending		Comparatives	
	fortis, forte - strong		ācer, ācris, ācre - sharp		potēns - powerful		fortior, fortius - stronger	
	M&F	N	M&F	N	M&F	N	M&F	N
Sing								
nom	fortis	forte	ācer, ācris	ācre	potēns		fortior	fortius
gen	fortis		ācris		potentis		fortiōris	
dat	fortī		ācrī		potentī		fortiōrī	
acc	fortem	forte	ācrem	ācre	potentem	potēns	fortiōrem	fortius
abl	fortī		ācrī		potentī		fortiōre	
Plu								
nom	fortēs, -īs	fortia	ācrēs	ācria	potentēs	potentia	fortiōrēs	fortiōra
gen	fortium		ācrium		potentium		fortiōrum	
dat	fortibus		ācribus		potentibus		fortiōribus	
acc	fortēs, -īs	fortia	ācrēs, -īs	ācria	potentēs, -īs	potentia	fortiōrēs	fortiōra
abl	fortibus		ācribus		potentibus		fortiōribus	

Regular Comparison of Adjectives

Positive	Comparative	Superlative
altus, -a, -um - high	altior, altius - higher	altissimus, -a, -um - highest
fortis, forte - strong	fortior, fortius - stronger	fortissimus, -a, -um - strongest
fēlīx, felicis - happy	fēlīcior, fēlīcius - happier	fēlīcissimus, -a, -um - happiest
facilis, facile - easy	facilior, facilius - easier	facillimus, -a, -um - easiest
līber, -era, -erum - free	līberior, līberius - freer	līberrimus, -a, -um - freest
pulcher, -chra, -chrum - beautiful	pulchrior, pulchrius - more beautiful	pulcherrimus, -a, -um - most beautiful
ācer, ācris, ācre - sharp	ācrior, ācrius - sharper	ācerrimus, -a, -um - sharpest

Irregular Comparison of Adjectives

Positive	Comparative	Superlative
bonus, -a, -um - good	melior, melius - better	optimus, -a, -um - best
magnus, -a, um - great	maior, maius - greater	maximus, -a, -um - greatest
malus, -a, -um - bad	peior, peius - worse	pessimus, -a, -um - worst
multus, -a, -um - much	——, plūs - more	plūrimus, -a, -um - most
parvus, -a, -um - small	minor, minus - smaller	minimus, -a, -um - smallest
(prae, prō)	prior, prius - former	prīmus, -a, -um - first
superus, -a, -um - above	superior, superius - higher	summus (suprēmus), -a, -um - highest

ADVERBS

Formation of Adverbs

Most adverbs are derived from adjectives. To make an adverb from a first and second declension adjective, add **-ē** to the base of the adjective (the masculine genitive singular minus the **-ī**). To make an adverb from a third declension adjective, add **-iter** to the base (the masculine genitive singular minus the **-is**). If the base ends in **-nt-**, however, you only add **-er**.

Adjective	Adverb
cārus - dear	cārē - dearly
līber - free	līberē - freely
pulcher - beautiful	pulchrē - beautifully
fortis - strong, brave	fortiter - bravely
ācer - sharp, fierce	ācriter - fiercely
levis - light	leviter - lightly
sapiēns - wise	sapienter - wisely

Comparison of Adverbs

For most adverbs, the comparative form is the same as the neuter comparative of the adjective. To form the superlative adverb, you add **-ē** to the base of the superlative adjective (just as with any first and second declension adjective).

Regular Comparison of Adverbs

Adverb	Comparative	Superlative
cārē	cārius	cārissimē
pulchrē	pulchrius	pulcherrimē
ācriter	ācrius	ācerrimē
leviter	levius	levissimē
sapienter	sapientius	sapientissimē
facile	facilius	facillimē

Irregular Comparison of Adverbs

Adverb	Comparative	Superlative
bene - well	melius - better	optimē - best
male - badly	peius - worse	pessimē - worst
multum - much	plūs - more (quantity)	plūrimum - most
magnopere - greatly	magis - more (quality)	maximē - greatest
parum - little	minus - less	minimē - least
(prō)	prius - before, earlier	prīmum - first
diū - a long time	diūtius - a longer time	diūtissimē - the longest, a very long time

PRONOUNS

Personal Pronouns

The first and second person personal pronouns correspond to the English pronouns I, me, and you. In the genitive plural, **nostrum** and **vestrum** are generally used as partitive genitives, while **nostrī** and **vestrī** are usually used as objective genitives. For the third person personal pronoun, use the demonstrative pronoun, **is, ea, id.**

	First Person	Second Person
Sing		
nom/voc	ego	tū
gen	meī	tuī
dat	mihi	tibi
acc	mē	tē
abl	mē	tē
Plu		
nom/voc	nōs	vōs
gen	nostrum/nostrī	vestrum/vestrī
dat	nōbīs	vōbīs
acc	nōs	vōs
abl	nōbīs	vōbīs

Reflexive Pronouns

Reflexive pronouns refer back to (or reflect back on) the subject. They do not have any nominative forms because they reflect back on the subject, mentioned earlier in the sentence. Only the forms for the third person reflexive pronoun are given here; the first and second person reflexive pronouns are the same as the personal pronouns (minus the nominative).

	Third Person
Sing	
gen	suī - of himself, herself, itself
dat	sibi
acc	sē or sēsē
abl	sē or sēsē
Plu	
gen	suī
dat	sibi
acc	sē or sēsē
abl	sē or sēsē

Grammatical Appendix

Demonstrative Pronouns

hic, haec, hoc - this

Sing	Masculine	Feminine	Neuter
nom	hic	haec	hoc
gen	huius	huius	huius
dat	huic	huic	huic
acc	hunc	hanc	hoc
abl	hōc	hāc	hōc
Plu			
nom	hī	hae	haec
gen	hōrum	hārum	hōrum
dat	hīs	hīs	hīs
acc	hōs	hās	haec
abl	hīs	hīs	hīs

ille, illa, illud - that

Sing	Masculine	Feminine	Neuter
nom	ille	illa	illud
gen	illīus	illīus	illīus
dat	illī	illī	illī
acc	illum	illam	illud
abl	illō	illā	illō
Plu			
nom	illī	illae	illa
gen	illōrum	illārum	illōrum
dat	illīs	illīs	illīs
acc	illōs	illās	illa
abl	illīs	illīs	illīs

is, ea, id - this, that, he, she, it

Sing	Masculine	Feminine	Neuter
nom	is	ea	id
gen	eius	eius	eius
dat	eī	eī	eī
acc	eum	eam	id
abl	eō	eā	eō
Plu			
nom	eī or iī	eae	ea
gen	eōrum	eārum	eōrum
dat	eīs or iīs	eīs or iīs	eīs or iīs
acc	eōs	eās	ea
abl	eīs or iīs	eīs or iīs	eīs or iīs

iste, ista, istud - that, that of yours (pejorative)

Sing	Masculine	Feminine	Neuter
nom	iste	ista	istud
gen	istīus	istīus	istīus
dat	istī	istī	istī
acc	istum	istam	istud
abl	istō	istā	istō
Plu			
nom	istī	istae	ista
gen	istōrum	istārum	istōrum
dat	istīs	istīs	istīs
acc	istōs	istās	ista
abl	istīs	istīs	istīs

īdem, eadem, idem - the same

Sing	Masculine	Feminine	Neuter
nom	īdem	eadem	idem
gen	eiusdem	eiusdem	eiusdem
dat	eīdem	eīdem	eīdem
acc	eundem	eandem	idem
abl	eōdem	eādem	eōdem
Plu			
nom	eīdem or iīdem	eaedem	eadem
gen	eōrundem	eārundem	eōrundem
dat	eīsdem	eīsdem	eīsdem
acc	eōsdem	eāsdem	eadem
abl	eīsdem	eīsdem	eīsdem

Intensive Pronoun

ipse, ipsa, ipsum - myself, yourself, himself, herself, itself

Sing	Masculine	Feminine	Neuter
nom	ipse	ipsa	ipsum
gen	ipsīus	ipsīus	ipsīus
dat	ipsī	ipsī	ipsī
acc	ipsum	ipsam	ipsum
abl	ipsō	ipsā	ipsō
Plu			
nom	ipsī	ipsae	ipsa
gen	ipsōrum	ipsārum	ipsōrum
dat	ipsīs	ipsīs	ipsīs
acc	ipsōs	ipsās	ipsa
abl	ipsīs	ipsīs	ipsīs

Relative Pronoun

quī, quae, quod - who, which

Sing	Masculine	Feminine	Neuter
nom	quī	quae	quod
gen	cuius	cuius	cuius
dat	cui	cui	cui
acc	quem	quam	quod
abl	quō	quā	quō
Plu			
nom	quī	quae	quae
gen	quōrum	quārum	quōrum
dat	quibus	quibus	quibus
acc	quōs	quās	quae
abl	quibus	quibus	quibus

Interrogative Pronoun

The plural of the interrogative pronoun is the same as that of the relative pronoun.

quis, quid - who?, what?

Sing	Masculine and Feminine	Neuter
nom	quis	quid
gen	cuius	cuius
dat	cui	cui
acc	quem	quid
abl	quō	quō

VERBS

Active Voice—Indicative Mood

Present

Sing	1st conj	2nd conj	3rd conj	3rd -io conj	4th conj
1st	amō	moneō	dūcō	capiō	audiō
2nd	amās	monēs	dūcis	capis	audīs
3rd	amat	monet	dūcit	capit	audit
Plu					
1st	amāmus	monēmus	dūcimus	capimus	audīmus
2nd	amātis	monētis	dūcitis	capitis	audītis
3rd	amant	monent	dūcunt	capiunt	audiunt

Grammatical Appendix

Imperfect

Sing	1st conj	2nd conj	3rd conj	3rd -io conj	4th conj
1st	amābam	monēbam	dūcēbam	capiēbam	audiēbam
2nd	amābās	monēbās	dūcēbās	capiēbās	audiēbās
3rd	amābat	monēbat	dūcēbat	capiēbat	audiēbat
Plu					
1st	amābāmus	monēbāmus	dūcēbāmus	capiēbāmus	audiēbāmus
2nd	amābātis	monēbātis	dūcēbātis	capiēbātis	audiēbātis
3rd	amābant	monēbant	dūcēbant	capiēbant	audiēbant

Future

Sing	1st conj	2nd conj	3rd conj	3rd -io conj	4th conj
1st	amābō	monēbō	dūcam	capiam	audiam
2nd	amābis	monēbis	dūcēs	capiēs	audiēs
3rd	amābit	monēbit	dūcet	capiet	audiet
Plu					
1st	amābimus	monēbimus	dūcēmus	capiēmus	audiēmus
2nd	amābitis	monēbitis	dūcētis	capiētis	audiētis
3rd	amābunt	monēbunt	dūcent	capient	audient

Perfect

Sing	1st conj	2nd conj	3rd conj	3rd -io conj	4th conj
1st	amāvī	monuī	dūxī	cēpī	audīvī
2nd	amāvistī	monuistī	dūxistī	cēpistī	audīvistī
3rd	amāvit	monuit	dūxit	cēpit	audīvit
Plu					
1st	amāvimus	monuimus	dūximus	cēpimus	audīvimus
2nd	amāvistis	monuistis	dūxistis	cēpistis	audīvistis
3rd	amāvērunt	monuērunt	dūxērunt	cēpērunt	audīvērunt

Pluperfect

Sing	1st conj	2nd conj	3rd conj	3rd -io conj	4th conj
1st	amāveram	monueram	dūxeram	cēperam	audīveram
2nd	amāverās	monuerās	dūxerās	cēperās	audīverās
3rd	amāverat	monuerat	dūxerat	cēperat	audīverat
Plu					
1st	amāverāmus	monuerāmus	dūxerāmus	cēperāmus	audīverāmus
2nd	amāverātis	monuerātis	dūxerātis	cēperātis	audīverātis
3rd	amāverant	monuerant	dūxerant	cēperant	audīverant

Future Perfect

Sing	1st conj	2nd conj	3rd conj	3rd -io conj	4th conj
1st	amāverō	monuerō	dūxerō	cēperō	audīverō
2nd	amāveris	monueris	dūxeris	cēperis	audīveris
3rd	amāverit	monuerit	dūxerit	cēperit	audīverit
Plu					
1st	amāverimus	monuerimus	dūxerimus	cēperimus	audīverimus
2nd	amāveritis	monueritis	dūxeritis	cēperitis	audīveritis
3rd	amāverint	monuerint	dūxerint	cēperint	audīverint

Active Voice—Subjunctive Mood

Present

Sing	1st conj	2nd conj	3rd conj	3rd -io conj	4th conj
1st	amem	moneam	dūcam	capiam	audiam
2nd	amēs	moneās	dūcās	capiās	audiās
3rd	amet	moneat	dūcat	capiat	audiat
Plu					
1st	amēmus	moneāmus	dūcāmus	capiāmus	audiāmus
2nd	amētis	moneātis	dūcātis	capiātis	audiātis
3rd	ament	moneant	dūcant	capiant	audiant

Imperfect

Sing	1st conj	2nd conj	3rd conj	3rd -io conj	4th conj
1st	amārem	monērem	dūcerem	caperem	audīrem
2nd	amārēs	monērēs	dūcerēs	capierēs	audīrēs
3rd	amāret	monēret	dūceret	caperet	audīret
Plu					
1st	amārēmus	monērēmus	dūcerēmus	caperēmus	audīrēmus
2nd	amārētis	monērētis	dūcerētis	caperētis	audīrētis
3rd	amārent	monērent	dūcerent	caperent	audīrent

Perfect

Sing	1st conj	2nd conj	3rd conj	3rd -io conj	4th conj
1st	amāverim	monuerim	dūxerim	cēperim	audīverim
2nd	amāverīs	monuerīs	dūxerīs	cēperīs	audīverīs
3rd	amāverit	monuerit	dūxerit	cēperit	audīverit
Plu					
1st	amāverīmus	monuerīmus	dūxerīmus	cēperīmus	audīverīmus
2nd	amāverītis	monuerītis	dūxerītis	cēperītis	audīverītis
3rd	amāvērint	monuerint	dūxerint	cēperint	audīverint

Pluperfect

Sing	1st conj	2nd conj	3rd conj	3rd -io conj	4th conj
1st	amāvissem	monuissem	dūxissem	cēpissem	audīvissem
2nd	amāvissēs	monuissēs	dūxissēs	cēpissēs	audīvissēs
3rd	amāvisset	monuisset	dūxisset	cēpisset	audīvisset
Plu					
1st	amāvissēmus	monuissēmus	dūxissēmus	cēpissēmus	audīvissēmus
2nd	amāvissētis	monuissētis	dūxissētis	cēpissētis	audvissētis
3rd	amāvissent	monuissent	dūxissent	cēpissent	audīvissent

Present Active Imperative

Sing	1st conj	2nd conj	3rd conj	3rd -io conj	4th conj
2nd	amā	monē	dūc*	cape	audī
Plu					
2nd	amāte	monēte	dūcite	capite	audīte

*Irregular. The present imperative of most third conjugation verbs ends in -e: scrībe, rege, crede, etc. There are only four third conjugation verbs that regularly drop the -e: dīc "say," dūc "lead," fac "do," and fer "bring."

Infinitives

Active	1st conj	2nd conj	3rd conj	3rd -io conj	4th conj
present	amāre	monēre	dūcere	capere	audīre
perfect	amāvisse	monuisse	dūxisse	cēpisse	audīvisse
future	amātūrus esse	monitūrus esse	ductūrus esse	captūrus esse	audītūrus esse
Passive					
present	amāri	monēri	dūcī	capī	audīrī
perfect	amātus esse	monitus esse	ductus esse	captus esse	audītus esse
future	amātum īrī	monitum īrī	ductum īrī	captum īrī	audītum īrī

Participles

Active	1st conj	2nd conj	3rd conj	3rd -io conj	4th conj
present	amāns	monēns	dūcēns	capiēns	audiēns
future	amātūrus	monitūrus	ductūrus	captūrus	audītūrus
Passive					
perfect	amātus	monitus	ductus	captus	audītus
future	amandus	monendus	dūcendus	capiendus	audiendus

Passive Voice—Indicative Mood

Present

Sing	1st conj	2nd conj	3rd conj	3rd -io conj	4th conj
1st	amor	moneor	dūcor	capior	audior
2nd	amāris (-re)	monēris (-re)	dūceris (-re)	caperis (-re)	audīris (-re)
3rd	amātur	monētur	dūcitur	capitur	audītur
Plu					
1st	amāmur	monēmur	dūcimur	capimur	audīmur
2nd	amāminī	monēminī	dūciminī	capiminī	audīminī
3rd	amantur	monentur	dūcuntur	capiuntur	audiuntur

Imperfect

Sing	1st conj	2nd conj	3rd conj	3rd -io conj	4th conj
1st	amābar	monēbar	dūcēbar	capiēbar	audiēbar
2nd	amābāris (-re)	monēbāris (-re)	dūcēbāris (-re)	capiēbāris (-re)	audiēbāris (-re)
3rd	amābātur	monēbātur	dūcēbātur	capiēbātur	audiēbātur
Plu					
1st	amābāmur	monēbāmur	dūcēbāmur	capiēbāmur	audiēbāmur
2nd	amābāminī	monēbāminī	dūcēbāminī	capiēbāminī	audiēbāminī
3rd	amābantur	monēbantur	dūcēbantur	capiēbantur	audiēbantur

Future

Sing	1st conj	2nd conj	3rd conj	3rd -io conj	4th conj
1st	amābor	monēbor	dūcar	capiar	audiar
2nd	amāberis (-re)	monēberis (-re)	dūcēris (-re)	capiēris (-re)	audiēris (-re)
3rd	amābitur	monēbitur	dūcētur	capiētur	audiētur
Plu					
1st	amābimur	monēbimur	dūcēmur	capiēmur	audiēmur
2nd	amābiminī	monēbiminī	dūcēminī	capiēminī	audiēminī
3rd	amābuntur	monēbuntur	dūcentur	capientur	audientur

Perfect

Sing	1st conj	2nd conj	3rd conj	3rd -io conj	4th conj
1st	amātus sum	monitus sum	ductus sum	captus sum	audītus sum
2nd	amātus es	monitus es	ductus es	captus es	audītus es
3rd	amātus est	monitus est	ductus est	captus est	audītus est
Plu					
1st	amātī sumus	monitī sumus	ductī sumus	captī sumus	audītī sumus
2nd	amātī estis	monitī estis	ductī estis	captī estis	audītī estis
3rd	amātī sunt	monitī sunt	ductī sunt	captī sunt	audītī sunt

Pluperfect

Sing	1st conj	2nd conj	3rd conj	3rd -io conj	4th conj
1st	amātus eram	monitus eram	ductus eram	captus eram	audītus eram
2nd	amātus erās	monitus erās	ductus erās	captus erās	audītus erās
3rd	amātus erat	monitus erat	ductus erat	captus erat	audītus erat
Plu					
1st	amātī erāmus	monitī erāmus	ductī erāmus	captī erāmus	audītī erāmus
2nd	amātī erātis	monitī erātis	ductī erātis	captī erātis	audītī erātis
3rd	amātī erant	monuitī erant	dūctī erant	captī erant	audītī erant

Future Perfect

Sing	1st conj	2nd conj	3rd conj	3rd -io conj	4th conj
1st	amātus erō	monitus erō	ductus erō	captus erō	audītus erō
2nd	amātus eris	monitus eris	ductus eris	captus eris	audītus eris
3rd	amātus erit	monitus erit	ductus erit	captus erit	audītus erit
Plu					
1st	amātī erimus	monitī erimus	ductī erimus	captī erimus	audītī erimus
2nd	amātī eritis	monitī eritis	ductī eritis	captī eritis	audītī eritis
3rd	amātī erunt	monitī erunt	ductī erunt	captī erunt	audītī erunt

Passive Voice—Subjunctive Mood

Present

Sing	1st conj	2nd conj	3rd conj	3rd -io conj	4th conj
1st	amer	monear	dūcar	capiar	audiar
2nd	amēris (-re)	moneāris (-re)	dūcāris (-re)	capiāris (-re)	audiāris (-re)
3rd	amētur	moneātur	dūcātur	capiātur	audiātur
Plu					
1st	amēmur	moneāmur	dūcāmur	capiāmur	audiāmur
2nd	amēminī	moneāminī	dūcāminī	capiāminī	audiāminī
3rd	amentur	moneantur	dūcantur	capiantur	audiantur

Imperfect

Sing	1st conj	2nd conj	3rd conj	3rd -io conj	4th conj
1st	amārer	monērer	dūcerer	caperer	audīrer
2nd	amārēris (-re)	monērēris (-re)	dūcerēris (-re)	caperēris (-re)	audīrēris (-re)
3rd	amārētur	monērētur	dūcerētur	caperētur	audīrētur
Plu					
1st	amārēmur	monērēmur	dūcerēmur	caperēmur	audīrēmur
2nd	amārēminī	monērēminī	dūcerēminī	caperēminī	audīrēminī
3rd	amārentur	monērentur	dūcerentur	caperentur	audīrentur

Perfect

Sing	1st conj	2nd conj	3rd conj	3rd -io conj	4th conj
1st	amātus sim	monitus sim	ductus sim	captus sim	audītus sim
2nd	amātus sīs	monitus sīs	ductus sīs	captus sīs	audītus sīs
3rd	amātus sit	monitus sit	ductus sit	captus sit	audītus sit
Plu					
1st	amātī sīmus	monitī sīmus	ductī sīmus	captī sīmus	audītī sīmus
2nd	amātī sītis	monitī sītis	ductī sītis	captī sītis	audītī sītis
3rd	amātī sint	monitī sint	dūctī sint	captī sint	audītī sint

Pluperfect

Sing	1st conj	2nd conj	3rd conj	3rd -io conj	4th conj
1st	amātus essem	monitus essem	ductus essem	captus essem	audītus essem
2nd	amātus essēs	monitus essēs	ductus essēs	captus essēs	audītus essēs
3rd	amātus esset	monitus esset	ductus esset	captus esset	audītus esset
Plu					
1st	amātī essēmus	monitī essēmus	ductī essēmus	captī essēmus	audītī essēmus
2nd	amātī essētis	monitī essētis	ductī essētis	captī essētis	audītī essētis
3rd	amātī essent	monitī essent	ductī essent	captī essent	audītī essent

Deponent Verbs

Present

Sing	1st conj	2nd conj	3rd conj	3rd -io conj	4th conj
1st	cōnor	polliceor	sequor	prōgredior	partior
2nd	cōnāris (-re)	pollicēris (-re)	sequeris (-re)	prōgrederis (-re)	partīris (-re)
3rd	cōnātur	pollicētur	sequitur	prōgreditur	partītur
Plu					
1st	cōnāmur	pollicēmur	sequimur	prōgredimur	partīmur
2nd	cōnāminī	pollicēminī	sequiminī	prōgrediminī	partīminī
3rd	cōnantur	pollicentur	sequuntur	prōgrediuntur	partiuntur

Imperfect

Sing	1st conj	2nd conj	3rd conj	3rd -io conj	4th conj
1st	cōnābar	pollicēbar	sequēbar	prōgrediēbar	partiēbar
2nd	cōnābāris (-re)	pollicēbāris (-re)	sequēbāris (-re)	prōgrediēbāris (-re)	partiēbāris (-re)
3rd	cōnābātur	pollicēbātur	sequēbātur	prōgrediēbātur	partiēbātur
Plu					
1st	cōnābāmur	pollicēbāmur	sequēbāmur	prōgrediēbāmur	partiēbāmur
2nd	cōnābāminī	pollicēbāminī	sequēbāminī	prōgrediēbāminī	partiēbāminī
3rd	cōnābantur	pollicēbantur	sequēbantur	prōgrediēbantur	partiēbantur

Future

Sing	1st conj	2nd conj	3rd conj	3rd -io conj	4th conj
1st	cōnābor	pollicēbor	sequar	prōgrediar	partiar
2nd	cōnāberis (-re)	pollicēberis (-re)	sequēris (-re)	prōgrediēris (-re)	partiēris (-re)
3rd	cōnābitur	pollicēbitur	sequētur	prōgrediētur	partiētur
Plu					
1st	cōnābimur	pollicēbimur	sequēmur	prōgrediēmur	partiēmur
2nd	cōnābiminī	pollicēbiminī	sequēminī	prōgrediēminī	partiēminī
3rd	cōnābuntur	pollicēbuntur	sequentur	prōgredientur	partientur

Perfect

Sing	1st conj	2nd conj	3rd conj	3rd -io conj	4th conj
1st	cōnātus sum	pollicitus sum	secūtus sum	prōgressus sum	partitus sum
2nd	cōnātus es	pollicitus es	secūtus es	prōgressus es	partitus es
3rd	cōnātus est	pollicitus est	secūtus est	prōgressus est	partitus est
Plu					
1st	cōnātī sumus	pollicitī sumus	secūtī sumus	prōgressī sumus	partitī sumus
2nd	cōnātī estis	pollicitī estis	secūtī estis	prōgressī estis	partitī estis
3rd	cōnātī sunt	pollicitī sunt	secūtī sunt	prōgressī sunt	partitī sunt

Pluperfect

Sing	1st conj	2nd conj	3rd conj	3rd -io conj	4th conj
1st	cōnātus eram	pollicitus eram	secūtus eram	prōgressus eram	partītus eram
2nd	cōnātus erās	pollicitus erās	secūtus erās	prōgressus erās	partītus erās
3rd	cōnātus erat	pollicitus erat	secūtus erat	prōgressus erat	partītus erat
Plu					
1st	cōnātī erāmus	pollicitī erāmus	secūtī erāmus	prōgressī erāmus	partītī erāmus
2nd	cōnātī erātis	pollicitī erātis	secūtī erātis	prōgressī erātis	partītī erātis
3rd	cōnātī erant	pollicitī erant	secūtī erant	prōgressī erant	partītī erant

Future Perfect

Sing	1st conj	2nd conj	3rd conj	3rd -io conj	4th conj
1st	cōnātus erō	pollicitus erō	secūtus erō	prōgressus erō	partītus erō
2nd	cōnātus eris	pollicitus eris	secūtus eris	prōgressus eris	partītus eris
3rd	cōnātus erit	pollicitus erit	secūtus erit	prōgressus erit	parītus erit
Plu					
1st	cōnātī erimus	pollicitī erimus	secūtī erimus	prōgressī erimus	partītī erimus
2nd	cōnātī eritis	pollicitī eritis	secūtī eritis	prōgressī eritis	partītī eritis
3rd	cōnātī erunt	pollicitī erunt	secūtī erunt	prōgressī erunt	partītī erunt

For the subjunctive forms of deponent verbs see the passive subjunctive forms of the paradigm verbs (**amō, moneō, dūcō, capiō,** and **audiō**).

IRREGULAR VERBS

sum, esse, fuī, futūrus - to be

Indicative Mood

Sing	Present	Imperfect	Future	Perfect	Pluperfect	Future Perfect
1st	sum	eram	erō	fuī	fueram	fuerō
2nd	es	erās	eris	fuistī	fuerās	fueris
3rd	est	erat	erit	fuit	fuerat	fuerit
Plu						
1st	sumus	erāmus	erimus	fuimus	fuerāmus	fuerimus
2nd	estis	erātis	eritis	fuistis	fuerātis	fueritis
3rd	sunt	erant	erunt	fuērunt	fuerant	fuerint

Subjunctive Mood

Sing	Present	Imperfect	Perfect	Pluperfect
1st	sim	essem	fuerim	fuissem
2nd	sīs	essēs	fuerīs	fuissēs
3rd	sit	esset	fuerit	fuisset
Plu				
1st	sīmus	essēmus	fuerīmus	fuissēmus
2nd	sītis	essētis	fuerītis	fuissētis
3rd	sint	essent	fuerint	fuissent

Present Imperative

2nd sing	es
2nd plu	este

Participle

Future	futūrus

Infinitives

Present	esse
Perfect	fuisse
Future	futūrus esse

possum, posse, potuī - to be able, can

Indicative Mood

Sing	Present	Imperfect	Future	Perfect	Pluperfect	Future Perfect
1st	possum	poteram	poterō	potuī	potueram	potuerō
2nd	potes	poterās	poteris	potuistī	potuerās	potueris
3rd	potest	poterat	poterit	potuit	potuerat	potuerit
Plu						
1st	possumus	poterāmus	poterimus	potuimus	potuerāmus	potuerimus
2nd	potestis	poterātis	poteritis	potuistis	potuerātis	potueritis
3rd	possunt	poterant	poterunt	potuērunt	potuerant	potuerint

Subjunctive Mood

Sing	Present	Imperfect	Perfect	Pluperfect
1st	possim	possem	potuerim	potuissem
2nd	possis	possēs	potuerīs	potuissēs
3rd	possit	posset	potuerit	potuisset
Plu				
1st	possīmus	possēmus	potuerīmus	potuissēmus
2nd	possītis	possētis	potuerītis	potuissētis
3rd	possint	possent	potuerint	potuissent

Participle

Present	potēns

Infinitives

Present	posse
Perfect	potuisse

volō, velle, voluī - to wish, be willing

Indicative Mood

Sing	Present	Imperfect	Future	Perfect	Pluperfect	Future Perfect
1st	volō	volēbam	volam	voluī	volueram	voluerō
2nd	vīs	volēbās	volēs	voluistī	voluerās	volueris
3rd	vult	volēbat	volet	voluit	voluerat	voluerit
Plu						
1st	volumus	volēbāmus	volēmus	voluimus	voluerāmus	voluerimus
2nd	vultis	volēbātis	volētis	voluistis	voluerātis	volueritis
3rd	volunt	volēbant	volent	voluērunt	voluerant	voluerint

Subjunctive Mood

Sing	Present	Imperfect	Perfect	Pluperfect
1st	velim	vellem	voluerim	voluissem
2nd	velīs	vellēs	voluerīs	voluissēs
3rd	velit	vellet	voluerit	voluisset
Plu				
1st	velīmus	vellēmus	voluerīmus	voluissēmus
2nd	velītis	vellētis	voluerītis	voluissētis
3rd	velint	vellent	voluerint	voluissent

Participle

Present	volēns

Infinitives

Present	velle
Perfect	voluisse

nōlō, nōlle, noluī - not to wish, be unwilling

Indicative Mood

Sing	Present	Imperfect	Future	Perfect	Pluperfect	Future Perfect
1st	nōlō	nōlēbam	nōlam	nōluī	nōlueram	nōluerō
2nd	nōn vīs	nōlēbās	nōlēs	nōluistī	nōluerās	nōlueris
3rd	nōn vult	nōlēbat	nōlet	nōluit	nōluerat	nōluerit
Plu						
1st	nōlumus	nōlēbāmus	nōlēmus	nōluimus	nōluerāmus	nōluerimus
2nd	nōn vultis	nōlēbātis	nōlētis	nōluistis	nōluerātis	nōlueritis
3rd	nōlunt	nōlēbant	nōlent	nōluērunt	nōluerant	nōluerint

Subjunctive Mood

Sing	Present	Imperfect	Perfect	Pluperfect
1st	nōlim	nōllem	nōluerim	nōluissem
2nd	nōlīs	nōllēs	nōluerīs	nōluissēs
3rd	nōlit	nōllet	nōluerit	nōluisset
Plu				
1st	nōlīmus	nōllēmus	nōluerīmus	nōluissēmus
2nd	nōlītis	nōllētis	nōluerītis	nōluissētis
3rd	nōlint	nōllent	nōluerint	nōluissent

Participle

Present	nōlēns

Infinitives

Present	nōlle
Perfect	nōluisse

mālō, mālle, māluī - to prefer

Indicative Mood

Sing	Present	Imperfect	Future	Perfect	Pluperfect	Future Perfect
1st	mālō	mālēbam	mālam	māluī	mālueram	māluerō
2nd	māvīs	mālēbās	mālēs	māluistī	māluerās	mālueris
3rd	māvult	mālēbat	mālet	māluit	māluerat	māluerit
Plu						
1st	mālumus	mālēbāmus	mālēmus	māluimus	māluerāmus	māluerimus
2nd	māvultis	mālēbātis	mālētis	māluistis	māluerātis	mālueritis
3rd	mālunt	mālēbant	mālent	māluērunt	māluerant	māluerint

Subjunctive Mood

Sing	Present	Imperfect	Perfect	Pluperfect
1st	mālim	māllem	māluerim	māluissem
2nd	mālīs	māllēs	māluerīs	māluissēs
3rd	mālit	māllet	māluerit	māluisset
Plu				
1st	mālīmus	māllēmus	māluerīmus	māluissēmus
2nd	mālītis	māllētis	māluerītis	māluissētis
3rd	mālint	māllent	māluerint	māluissent

Infinitives

Present	mālle
Perfect	māluisse

eō, īre, iī, itum - to go

Indicative Mood

Sing	Present	Imperfect	Future	Perfect	Pluperfect	Future Perfect
1st	eō	ībam	ībō	iī	ieram	ierō
2nd	īs	ībās	ībis	īstī	ierās	ieris
3rd	it	ībat	ībit	iit	ierat	ierit
Plu						
1st	īmus	ībāmus	ībimus	iimus	ierāmus	ierimus
2nd	ītis	ībātis	ībitis	īstis	ierātis	ieritis
3rd	eunt	ībant	ībunt	iērunt	ierant	ierint

Subjunctive Mood

Sing	Present	Imperfect	Perfect	Pluperfect
1st	eam	īrem	ierim	īssem
2nd	eās	īrēs	ierīs	īssēs
3rd	eat	īret	ierit	īsset
Plu				
1st	eāmus	īrēmus	ierīmus	īssēmus
2nd	eātis	īrētis	ierītis	īssētis
3rd	eānt	īrent	ierint	īssent

Present Imperative

2nd sing	ī
2nd plu	īte

Participles

Present	iēns, euntis
Future Active	itūrus
Future Passive	eundus

Infinitives

Present	īre
Perfect	īsse or īvisse
Future	itūrus esse

ferō, ferre, tulī, lātum - to bear, carry

Active Voice

Indicative Mood

Sing	Present	Imperfect	Future	Perfect	Pluperfect	Future Perfect
1st	ferō	ferēbam	feram	tulī	tuleram	tulerō
2nd	fers	ferēbās	ferēs	tulistī	tulerās	tuleris
3rd	fert	ferēbat	feret	tulit	tulerat	tulerit
Plu						
1st	ferimus	ferēbāmus	ferēmus	tulimus	tulerāmus	tulerimus
2nd	fertis	ferēbātis	ferētis	tulistis	tulerātis	tuleritis
3rd	ferunt	ferēbant	ferent	tulērunt	tulerant	tulerint

Subjunctive Mood

Sing	Present	Imperfect	Perfect	Pluperfect
1st	feram	ferrem	tulerim	tulissem
2nd	ferās	ferrēs	tulerīs	tulissēs
3rd	ferat	ferret	tulerit	tulisset
Plu				
1st	ferāmus	ferrēmus	tulerīmus	tulissēmus
2nd	ferātis	ferrētis	tulerītis	tulissētis
3rd	ferant	ferrent	tulerint	tulissent

Present Imperative

2nd sing	fer
2nd plu	ferte

Participles

	Active	Passive
Present	ferēns	
Perfect		lātus
Future	lātūrus	ferendus

Infinitives

	Active	Passive
Present	ferre	ferrī
Perfect	tulisse	lātus esse
Future	lātūrus esse	lātum īrī

Passive Voice

Indicative Mood

Sing	Present	Imperfect	Future	Perfect	Pluperfect	Future Perfect
1st	feror	ferēbar	ferar	lātus sum	lātus eram	lātus erō
2nd	ferris or -re	ferēbāris or -re	ferēris or -re	lātus es	lātus erās	lātus eris
3rd	fertur	ferēbātur	ferētur	lātus est	lātus erat	lātus erit
Plu						
1st	ferimur	ferēbāmur	ferēmur	lātī sumus	lātī erāmus	lātī erimus
2nd	feriminī	ferēbāminī	ferēminī	lātī estis	lātī erātis	lātī eritis
3rd	feruntur	ferēbantur	ferentur	lātī sunt	lātī erant	lātī erunt

Subjunctive Mood

Sing	Present	Imperfect	Perfect	Pluperfect
1st	ferar	ferrer	lātus sim	lātus essem
2nd	ferāris or -re	ferrēris or -re	lātus sīs	lātus essēs
3rd	ferātur	ferrētur	lātus sit	lātus esset
Plu				
1st	ferāmur	ferrēmur	lātī sīmus	lātī essēmus
2nd	ferāminī	ferrēminī	lātī sītis	lātī essētis
3rd	ferantur	ferrentur	lātī sint	lātī essent

fiō, fierī, factus sum - be made, be done, become

Indicative Mood

Sing	Present	Imperfect	Future	Perfect	Pluperfect	Future Perfect
1st	fīō	fīēbam	fīam	factus sum	factus eram	factus erō
2nd	fīs	fīēbās	fīēs	factus es	factus erās	factus eris
3rd	fit	fīēbat	fīet	factus est	factus erat	factus erit
Plu						
1st	fīmus	fīēbāmus	fīēmus	factī sumus	factī erāmus	factī erimus
2nd	fītis	fīēbātis	fīētis	factī estis	factī erātis	factī eritis
3rd	fīunt	fīēbant	fīent	factī sunt	factī erant	factī erunt

Subjunctive Mood

Sing	Present	Imperfect	Perfect	Pluperfect
1st	fīam	fierem	factus sim	factus essem
2nd	fīās	fierēs	factus sīs	factus essēs
3rd	fīat	fieret	factus sit	factus esset
Plu				
1st	fīāmus	fierēmus	factī sīmus	factī essēmus
2nd	fīātis	fierētis	factī sītis	factī essētis
3rd	fīant	fierent	factī sint	factī essent

Present Imperative

2nd sing	fī
2nd plu	fīte

Participles

Present	———
Perfect	factus
Future	faciendus

Infinitives

Present	fierī
Perfect	factus esse
Future	factum īrī

Latin-English Glossary

A

a, ab, prep. + abl. - from, away from; by (personal agent)
acer, acris, acre - sharp, keen, eager
  acrius, comp. adv - more keenly, more eagerly
ad, prep. + acc. - to, toward
aedificium, -i, n - a building
aedifico, aedificare, aedificavi, aedificatum - to build (something)
Aeneas, m - name of the Trojan hero Aeneas
  Aeneae, gen.; **Aenean** or **Aeneam**, acc.
ager, agri, m - a field
agnosco, agnoscere, agnovi, agnotum - to recognize, identify
ago, agere, egi, actum - to make, do
agricola, -ae, m - a farmer
Alba Longa - Alba Longa, a city in Italy
albus, -a, -um - white
aliqui, aliqua, aliquod, indef. pron. and adj.- some, any
alius, -a, -um - another
Allobroges, Allobrogum, m plu. - the Allobroges, a warlike tribe living in Gallia Narbonensis
ambulo, ambulare, ambulavi, ambulatum - to walk, travel
amicus, -i, m - a friend
amitto, amittere, amisi, amissum - to lose; lose by death
amo, amare, amavi, amatum - to love
Amulius, -i, m - Amulius, the younger brother of Numitor
Anchises, -ae, m - Anchises, father of Aeneas
ancilla, -ae, f - maidservant, handmaid, maid
animal, animalis, n - animal
animus, -i, m - the soul
annus, -i, m - a year
appello, appellare, appellavi, appellatum - to call, name
appropinquo, appropinquare, -avi, -atum - to approach
Aprilis, -is, adj. - of April; used to designate the month of April, with **mensis** understood
apud, pron. + acc. - at the house of, among
aranea, -ae, f - a spider
arbor, -oris, f - a tree
arena, -ae, f - sand; arena (a sandy place marked off for combat)
aro, arare, aravi, aratum - to plough
ars, artis, f - skill, art
ascendo, ascendere, ascendi, ascensum - to climb up, ascend
Asia, -ae, f - Asia
aspicio, aspicere, aspexi, aspectum - to look at, watch, observe, examine
Athenae, -arum, f plu. - Athens
Athenensis, -is, m - an Athenian
astrum, -i, n - a star
audio, audire, audivi, auditum - to hear
augurium -i, n - augury, a prediction of the future (or the gods' will) by interpreting the flight of birds
Augustus, Augusti, m - Caesar Augustus (Octavian)
aut, conjunct. - or
autem, conjunct. - but, however
auxilium, auxilii, n - help

B

baculum, -i, n - a stick, staff, walking-stick
barbarus, -i, m - a barbarian, foreigner
basio, basiare, basiavi, basiatum - to kiss
bellum, -i, n - a war
bellus, -a, -um - pretty
bene, adv. - well
bonus, -a, -um - good
bonus, -i, m - substantive - a good man
Britannia, -ae, f - Britain

C

cado, cadere, cecidi, casum - to fall
caelum, -i, n - the sky
Caesar, Caesaris, m - (Julius) Caesar
candidus, -a, -um - shining
canis, canis, m/f - dog
cano, canere, cecini, —— - to sing; of a musical instrument, to sound, resound (no 4th principal part)
capio, capere, cepi, captum - to take hold, seize
captivus, -i, m - a captive, prisoner
carcer, carceris, m - a prison
carmen, -inis, n - a poem, song
castellum, -i, n - a fort
castra, -orum, n. plu. - a military camp
Catullus, -i, m - Catullus (c. 84–54 BC), a poet of the late Republican period who wrote several

well-known poems to his on-again off-again girlfriend, Lesbia. In poem 5, Catullus asks Lesbia for many thousands of kisses.
causa, -ae, f - a cause, reason
    causā - in the ablative, **causa** becomes a preposition with the genitive (usually coming after its object) - for the sake of, for the purpose of
cedo, cedere, cessi, cessum, + dat - to yield, give place to
celeriter - quickly, hastily
cena, -ae, f - dinner
centurio, centurionis, m - centurion, commander of a century, captain
cibus, cibi, m - food
Cicero, Ciceronis, m - Cicero
cista, -ae, f - woven basket, box, chest
civilis, -e - civil, of citizens, civic
civis, -is, m - a citizen
clamo, -are, -avi, -atum - to call, cry out, shout aloud, complain aloud
clarus, -a, -um - famous; clear
    clarius, adv - more clearly
classis, -is, m - a fleet of ships
cognosco, cognoscere, cognovi, cognitum - to know, understand, recognize
cogo, cogere, coegi, coactum - to drive together, collect, congregate, convene, gather
comes, comitis, m/f - companion, associate, comrade
condo, condere, condidi, conditum - to build, found
conficio, conficere, confeci, confectum - to create, fashion, invent
coniuratio, -onis, f - a conspiracy, plot
conor, conari, conatus sum - to attempt, try, endeavor
constituo, constituere, constitui, constitutum - to decide
constrepo, constrepere, constrepui, constreptum - to make a loud noise
construo, construere, construxi, constructum - to build, construct
consul, consulis, m - a consul
consulo, consulere, consului, consultum - to consult
consumo, consumere, consumpsi, consumptum - to use, spend, consume
convenio, convenire, convēni, conventum - to come together; to come to a decision, agree
copia, -ae, f - ample supply, abundance
    copiae, -arum, f plu. - forces, troops, an army
coquo, coquere, coxi, coctum - to cook
coquus, -i, m - a cook
corroboro, corroborare, corroboravi, corroboratum - to strengthen, fortify, make strong
cras, adv - tomorrow
credo, credere, credidi, creditum - to believe
cresco, crescere, crevi, cretum - to grow, arise
Creusa, -ae, f - the wife of Aeneas
cum, prep. + gen. - with
cum, subord. conjunct. - when, since, although
cupiditas, cupiditatis, f - a desire
cupio, cupere, cupivi, cupitum - to wish, desire
cur, interrogative adv. - why?
curro, currere, cucurri, cursum - to run

D

decem - ten
dedecus, dedecoris, n - disgrace, dishonor, shame
defendo, defendere, defendi, defensum - to defend, guard, protect
defetiscor, defetisci, defessus sum - to become tired, grow weary
delego, deligere, delegi, delectum - to choose, select
deleo, delere, delevi, deletum - to destroy
despero, desperare, desperavi, desperatum - to lose hope, despair
deus, dei, m - a god; nom. plu., **dii**
dico, dicere, dixi, dictum - to say, tell
Dido, Didonis, f - Dido, the queen of Carthage in the *Aeneid* who falls in love with Aeneas
dies, diei, m - a day (this word is occasionally feminine)
discipulus, -i, m - a student
disco, discere, didici, ——— - to learn (no 4th principal part)
diu - a long time, for a long time
diutius, comp. adv. - for a longer time, for a very long time, for too long
do, dare, dedi, datum - to give, pay
doleo, dolere, dolui, doliturus - to grieve, lament
domi - locative case of domus - at home
dominus, -i, m - a master
domus, -ūs, f - a house, home (an irreg. 4th declension noun, with some 2nd declension endings)
dormio, dormire, dormivi, dormitum - to sleep
duco, ducere, duxi, ductum - to lead
dulcis, dulcis - sweet, pleasant
    dulciter, adv. - sweetly
duodecim, indecl. adj. - twelve
dux, ducis, m - a leader, military commander, general

Latin-English Glossary

E

educo, educare, educavi, educatum - to bring up, educate (do not confuse with **educo, educere**)
educo, educere, eduxi, eductum - to lead out (do not confuse with **educo, educare**)
effugio, effugere, effugi, effugitum - to flee, escape
ego, mei, mihi, me, me - I, me (1st pers. sing. pron.)
emo, emere, emi, emptus - to buy, purchase
eo, ire, ivi, itum - to go
epistula, -ae, f - a letter, epistle
equus, -i, m - a horse
Etruscus, -i, m - an Etruscan; the Etruscan were an ancient Italic ethnic group
Eurydice, -ēs, f - Eurydice, the wife of Orpheus who was killed by a snake; Orpheus got permission to bring her back from Hades, but he looked back at her too soon and she had to return.
ex, e, prep. + abl. - from, out of
excedo, excedere, excessi, excessum - to go out, depart
exeo, exire, exivi or exii, exitum - to go out from, depart from, leave, depart
exercitus, -ūs, m - an army
expello, -ere, expuli, expulsum - to drive out, eject, expel
experior, experiri, expertus sum - to experience; to try, test, prove
exploro, explorare, exploravi, exploratum - to examine, investigate, explore
exprimo, exprimere, expremi, expressum - to portray, describe, express

F

fabula, -ae, f - a story
facile, adv. - easily
facio, facere, feci, factum - to make, do
facinus, -oris, n - a crime
fateor, fateri, fassus sum - to confess, grant, acknowledge
fatum, -i, n - fate (literally, "that which has been spoken")
Faustulus, -i, m - Faustulus, the king's shepherd, who found Romulus and Remus and brought them up as his own sons
faveo, favere, favi, fauturus - to favor, be favorable toward, be well disposed toward
felix, felicis, adj - lucky, happy, fortunate, prosperous, successful
felēs, -īs, f - a cat
femina, -ae, f - a woman
fero, ferre, tuli, latum - to bear, carry, bring
ferox, -ocis - fierce, wild
ferus, -a, -um - wild, savage
fessus, -a, -um - tired
fidelis, fidele, adj. - faithful, trustworthy
filia, -ae, f - a daughter
filius, filii, m - a son
finio, finire, finivi, finitum - to finish
fio, fieri, factus sum - to become; also used as the passive of **facio** - to be turned into, be made
fleo, flere, flevi, fletum - to weep
foedus, -eris, n - a treaty
fortasse, adv. - perhaps
fortis, forte - strong, brave
fortiter, adv. - bravely
forum, -i, n - a forum
Forum, -i, n - the Forum at Rome, an open space between the Capitoline and Palatine hills, surrounded by shops, temples, and government buildings
frater, fratris, m - a brother
frumentum, -i, n - wheat, grain, harvested grain
fugio, fugere, fugi, fugitum - to flee from, run away from, avoid, escape
fur, furis, m - a thief
furor, furari, furatus sum - to steal

G

Galli, -orum, m plu. - the Gauls
Gallia, -ae, f - Gaul
gaudeo, gaudere, ———, gavisum - to rejoice, be glad (no 3rd principal part)
geminus, -a, -um - twin
gemma, -ae, f - a precious stone, jewel, gem
gero, gerere, gessi, gestum - to accomplish; to wage (war)
gladiator, -oris, m - one who fights with a sword (gladius), especially in the arena; gladiator
gladiatorius, -a, -um - gladiatorial, of gladiators
gladius, -i, m - a sword
Graecia, -ae, f - Greece
Graecus, -i, m - a Greek
gratia, -ae, f - favor, esteem; a favor, kindness; thanks, thankfulness
    gratiā - in the abl., with a preceding gen. - for the sake of
gravis, grave - heavy; serious, weighty, important

H

habeo, habere, habui, habitum - to have, hold; to deliver an oration
habito, habitare, habitavi, habitatum - freq. of **habeo** - to dwell, live in, reside

Helvetii, Helvetiorum, m plu. - the Helvetians, a Gallic tribe living in modern-day Switzerland
Hercules, Herculis, m - Hercules
hic, haec, hoc - this, that; plu.: these, those
hiems, hiemis, f - winter
historia, -ae, f - history
hodie, adv. - today
homo, hominis, m/f - a man, human being
hortus, -i, m - a garden
hostis, -is, m/f - usually plu. - enemy, foe, public enemy

I

iacio, iacere, ieci, iactum - to throw, hurl
ignis, ignis, m - fire
ille, illa, illud - that, those (plu.)
illudo, illudere, illusi, illusum - to mock, make fun of, ridicule
imperator, -oris, m - a general, commander
impero, imperare, imperavi, imperatum, + dat. pers. - to order, command
impetus, -ūs, m - an attack
impugno, impugnare, impugnavi, impugnatum - to attack
in - prep. + abl. - in; prep. + acc. - into
incipio, incipere, incepi, inceptum - to begin
incola, incolae, m/f - an inhabitant, resident
inde, adv. - of place: from that place, thence; of time: from that time on
infans, infantis, m/f - an infant, baby
inferi, -orum, m plu. - the dead, inhabitants of the underworld
   ad inferos - to the place where the dead people are, i.e., to the underworld
insula, -ae, f - an island
inter, prep. + acc. - between, among, during
interficio, interficere, interfeci, interfectum - to kill
invenio, -ire, inveni, inventum - to find, discover
ipse, ipsa, ipsum, intensive pron. - himself, herself, itself, themselves, etc.
irascor, irasci, iratus sum - to become angry
is, ea, id, weak demonstrative pron. - he/she/it/they, this/that
iste, ista, istud, demonstrative pron. (pejorative) - this, that, he, she, it
iter, itineris, n - a journey
iubeo, iubere, iussi, iussum - to order, command (takes acc. pers. + inf.)
iudicium, -i, n - judgment, decision
iustus, -a, -um - just
iuvenis, -is, m - a youth

Italia, -ae, f - Italy
itaque, conjunct. - and so, and accordingly

L

laboro, laborare, laboravi, laboratum - to work, labor
laetor, laetari, laetatus sum - to rejoice, feel happy, be glad
laetus, -a, -um - happy, glad
Larentia, -ae, f - Larentia the wife of Faustulus
Latini, -orum - the Latins, the people of Lavinium, named for Latinus
Latinus, -i, m - Latinus, king of the Latins and the father of Lavinia
latro, latrare, latravi, latratum - to bark
latro, latronis, m - a thief, robber
laudo, laudare, laudavi, laudatum - to praise
Lavinia, -ae, f - the wife of Aeneas
Lavinium, -i, n - the name of a city in Italy where the Latins lived
lectus, -i, m - a bed, couch
legatus, -i, m - an ambassador, envoy, legate; lieutenant, deputy, second-in-command
legio, legionis, f - a legion, a body of soldiers consisting of approx. 5,000–6,000 men
lego, legere, lexi, lectum - to read
leo, leonis, m - a lion
Lesbia, -ae, f - the name that Catullus gives to his on-again off-again girlfriend in many of his poems
lex, legis, f - a law
libenter, adv. - gladly, with pleasure
liber, libri, m - a book
liber, libera, liberum - free
liberi, liberorum, m plu. - children (the free young persons of the family)
libertas, -tatis, f - freedom
ligneus, -a, -um - wooden, made of wood
locus, -i, m - a place, region
longus, -a, -um - long
   longior, longius, comp. adj. - longer, rather long
loquor, loqui, locutus sum - to speak
ludus, ludi, m - a game; school
lupa, -ae, f - a she-wolf
lux, lucis, f - light
   prima lux - dawn (first light)
lyra, -ae, f - a lyre, a stringed instrument

M

magister, -tri, m - a teacher, master
magnitudo, -tudinis, f - greatness, large size; **magnitudo animi** - greatness of soul

magnopere - greatly
magnus, -a, -um - large, great (of size or value)
   maior, maius, comp. of magnus - larger, greater
malo, malle, malui, ——— - to prefer
   irreg. pres. subjunctive - **malim, malis, malit, malimus, malitis, malint**
malus, -a, -um - bad, wicked, evil
maneo, manere, mansi, mansum - to remain, stay
manes, manium, m plu. - a departed spirit, ghost, shade
manus, -ūs, f - a band, troop, company; a hand
mare, maris, n - the sea
Mars, Martis, m - Mars, the Roman god of war
mater, matris, f - a mother
melior, melius, comp. adj. of **bonus** - better
   melius, adv. - better
mens, mentis, f - mind
mensis, -is, m - a month
metuo, metuere, metui, ——— - to fear (no 4th principal part)
meus, mea, meum, possessive adj. - my
mihi - *see* **ego**
miles, -itis, m - a soldier
miror, mirari, miratus sum - to marvel (at), wonder
mitto, mittere, misi, missum - to send
moleste, adv. - with difficulty
   fero moleste - I am annoyed (I bear it with difficulty)
moneo, monere, monui, monitus - to warn
mons, montis, m - a mountain
morior, mori, mortuus sum - to die
moror, morari, moratus sum - to delay, tarry, wait, remain, linger
mors, mortis, f - death
moveo, movere, movi, motum - to move, set in motion
mox - soon
multus, -a, -um - much; plu. - many
munio, munire, munivi, munitum - to build, fortify
murus, -i, m - a wall, city wall

N

narro, narrare, narravi, narratum - to tell, narrate, report, explain
nascor, nasci, natus sum - to be born; to grow, arise, be in the early stages
nato, -are, -avi, -atum - to swim
nauta, -ae, m - a sailor
navigo, navigare, navigavi, navigatum - to sail, navigate
navis, -is, f - a ship
ne, conjunct. - in a command or purpose clause, it signals a negative command or purpose; in a fearing clause, it signals a positive fear
neco, necare, necavi, necatum - to kill, murder
negotium, -i, n - work, task
nepos, nepotis, m - a grandson
nescio, nescire, nescivi, ——— - to not know, be ignorant (no 4th principal part)
nihil, indecl. noun - nothing
nisi, unless, except, if not
nomen, nominis, n - a name
nos, nobis - we, us
noster, nostra, nostrum, possessive adj. - our
novus, -a, -um - new
nox, noctis, f - night (i-stem)
nubes, nubis, f - a cloud
Numitor, Numitoris, m - Numitor, the rightful king of Alba Longa, who was deposed by his brother, Amulius
numquam, adv. - never
nunc, adv. - now
nuntio, nuntiare, nuntiavi, nuntiatum - to announce
nuntius, -i, m - news, announcement; a messenger
nutrio, nutrire, nutrivi, nutritum - to suckle, nourish, nurse, feed

O

obscurus, -a, -um - dark
obsideo, obsidere, obsedi, obessesum - to besiege
obtineo, obtinere, obtinui, obtentum - to gain, acquire, obtain
occido, occidere, occidi, occasus - to fall; of the sun - to set
Odysseus, -i, m - Odysseus, hero of the *Odyssey*
offero, offerre, obtuli, oblatum - to offer
omen, ominis, n - an omen
omnis, -e, adj - every, all, the whole; plu. - all
   - plu. noun - all men, people, women, things
oppidum, -i, n - a town
oppugno, -are, -avi, -atum - to attack
opulentus, -a, -um - wealthy
opus, operis, n - work
oraculum, -i, n - an oracle, prophecy, divine pronouncement
orator, -oris, m - a speaker, orator
oro, orare, oravi, oratum - to speak; to beg, beseech, implore
Orpheus, -i, m - Orpheus, the husband of Eurydice and the greatest lyre-player of all time

P

paedagogus, -i, m - a pedagogue, slave who accompanied children to school
pareo, parere, parui, paritum + dat. - to obey
paro, parare, paravi, paratum - to prepare
partior, partiri, partitus sum - to share
parvus, -a, -um - little
pastor, -oris, m - a shepherd
pater, patris, m - a father
patior, pati, passus sum - to allow, suffer, endure
patria, -ae, m - native country, fatherland
paucus, -a, -um - a few (usu. plu.)
pax, pacis, f - peace
pecunia, -ae, f - money
perdo, perdere, perdidi, perditum - to lose (something)
peregrinus, -i, m - a foreigner, stranger
pereo, perire, perii, peritum - to die, perish
perficio, perficere, perfeci, perfectum - to complete, accomplish, perform
periculosus, -a, -um - dangerous
persuadeo, persuadere, persuasi, persuasum + dat. pers. - to persuade
pertimesco, pertimescere, pertimui, ——— - to be frightened, alarmed, fear greatly (no 4th principal part)
peto, petere, petivi, petitum - to seek; ask
philosophia, -ae, f - philosophy
piscor, piscari, piscatus sum - to fish, go fishing
pius, -a, -um - dutiful, loyal, conscientious, faithful
placeo, placere, placui, placitum + dat. pers. - to please
plaustrum, -i, n - wagon, cart
Pluto, -onis, m - Pluto, the god of the Underworld
poema, -atis, n - a poem
poeta, -ae, m - a poet
polliceor, polliceri, pollicitus sum - to promise
pono, ponere, posui, positum - to put, place
populus, -i, m - people, the people
porto, portare, portavi, portatum - bring, take, carry, convey
portus, -ūs, m - harbor, port
possum, posse, potui, ——— - to be able, can (no 4th principal part)
postea, adv. - later
postulo, postulare, -avi, -atum - ask for, demand, request
potens, potentis - powerful
potestas, potestatis, f - power, esp. political power
praeda, -ae, f - booty, spoil, plunder, stolen goods
premo, premere, pressi, pressum - to press
pretium, pretii, n - a prize, reward
prima lux - dawn (first light)
prius, comp. adv. - before, sooner, first
proficiscor, proficisci, profectus sum - to depart, set out
progredior, progredi, progressus sum - to go forward, advance
propter, prep. + acc. - on account of
provoco, provocare, provocavi, provocatum - to call forth; to challenge
prudens, prudentis - sensible, prudent, wise
publice, adv. - publicly
publicus, -a, -um - of the people, public
puella, -ae, f - a girl
puer, pueri, m - a boy
pugna, -ae, f - a battle
pugno, -are, pugnavi, pugnatum - to fight
pulcher, -ra, -rum - beautiful, handsome
  pulcherrimus, -a, -um - most beautiful (superlative)
purus, -a, -um - pure, chaste, undefiled

Q

quaero, quaere, quaesivi, quaesitum - to seek, ask for
quando - when
quare, interrogative adv. - why?
qui, quae, quod, relative pron. - who, which, what
quia, subord. conjunct. - because
quis, quid, interrogative pron. - who?, what?
quod, subord. conjunct. - because
quomodo, interrogative adv. - how?, in what manner?

R

recipio, recipere, recepi, receptum - to regain, recover, take back again
reddo, reddere, redidi, reditum, trans. verb - to give back, return, restore
redeo, redire, redivi, reditum, intrans. verb - to return, go back
regio, regionis, f - an area, region
regno, regnare, regnavi, regnatum - to reign, rule
regnum, -i, n - a kingdom
Remus, -i, m - Remus, brother of Romulus
res, rei, f - a thing, matter, affair
  res publica, -ae, f - the republic
respicio, respicere, respexi, respectum - to look back
rex, regis, m - a king
Rhea Silvia - the daughter of Numitor and the mother of Romulus and Remus
rogo, rogare, rogavi, rogatum - to ask
Roma, -ae, f - Rome

Romanus, -i, m - a Roman
Romulus, -i, m - Romulus, founder of Rome

S

sacculus, -i, m - a small bag or purse
sacerdos, -dotis, m/f - priest, priestess
saepe, adv. - often
sanctus, -a, -um, sacred, pure, holy, pious, just, upright, chaste
satis, indecl. adj. - enough
saxum, -i, n - a large stone, rock
scientia, -ae, f - knowledge, type of knowledge, field of knowledge
scio, scire, scivi, scitum - to know, understand, have knowledge of, be skilled in
scribo, scribere, scripsi, scriptum - to write
se - *see* **sui**
sed, conjunct. - but
sedeo, sedere, sedi, sessum - to sit, sit down
semper, adv. - always
senator, senatoris, m - a senator
senatus, -ūs, m - the senate, council of elders
senex, senis, m - an old man
sententia, -ae, f - opinion, judgment, decision
sequor, sequi, secutus sum - to follow
serius, comp. adv. - later
serpens, serpentis, m/f - a serpent, snake
servo, servare, servavi, servatum - to save, keep safe, protect; to watch, regard, pay attention to
servus, -i, m - a slave, servant
sex, indecl. adj. - six
si, subord. conjunct. - if; in an indirect question - whether
Sibylla, -ae, f - the Sibyl, a priestess of Apollo who can see the future
sidus, sideris, n - a star
signum, -i, n - a signal, sign
socius, socii, m - an ally
sodalis, -is, m/f - a comrade, companion, close friend
sol, solis, m - the sun
sonore, adv. - loudly
soror, sororis, f - a sister
specto, spectare, spectavi, spectatum - to look at, see, gaze at, view, behold, observe
spes, spei, f - hope
statua, -ae, f - a statue
sto, stare, steti, statum - to stand
stringo, stringere, strinxi, strinctum - to draw (one's sword), unsheathe
studeo, studere, studui, ——— + dat. - to study, give attention to (no 4th principal part)

stupeo, -ere, stupui, ——— - to be amazed or dumbfounded (no 4th principal part)
suavis, suave - sweet
sui, sibi, se, se - he, himself, they, themselves (3rd person reflexive pron., sing. and plu.)
sum, esse, fui, futurus - to be
supersum, superesse, superfui, ——— - to survive, remain alive (no 4th principal part)
suscipio, suscipere, suscepi, susceptum - to undertake, assume, begin
suscito, suscitare, suscitavi, suscitatum - to arouse (someone) from sleep; passive - to wake up
sustineo, sustinere, sustinui, sustentum - to hold up, bear up, sustain, maintain, endure, tolerate
suus, sua, suum - his own, her own, their own (3rd person reflexive possessive adj.)

T

taceo, tacere, tacui, tacitum - to be quiet, keep quiet
tam, adv. - so, so much
tamdiu, adv. - so long, for so long
tamen, subord. conjunct. - nevertheless, yet
tandem, adv. - eventually, finally, after some time
tantus, -a, -um - so, so great, of such a size
tantum, adv. - so much, to such an extent or degree
tempestas, -tatis, f - a storm
tempus, temporis, n - time
teneo, tenere, tenui, tentum - to hold, hold fast, keep
terreo, terrere, terrui, territum - to frighten, terrify (transitive verb)
thesaurus, -i, m - treasure; treasure house, treasury
Tiberis, -is, m - the Tiber River
timeo, timere, timui, ——— - to fear, be afraid (no 4th principal part)
timidus, -a, -um - frightened, fearful, afraid
totiens, adv. - so often, so many times
trado, tradere, tradidi, traditum - to hand over, give up; to betray
tragicus, -a, -um - tragic
traho, trahere, traxi, tractum - to drag, draw, haul
transeo, transire, transivi, transitum - to go over, cross
transilio, transilire, transilui, ——— - to jump over, leap over (no 4th principal part)
Troia, -ae, f - Troy, a city in ancient legend
Troianus, -i, m. - Trojan
tu, tui, tibi, te, te - you (2nd pers. sing. pron.)
turbo, turbare, turbavi, turbatum - to make a noise, disturb

U

ubi, interrogative adv. - where?
ullus, -a, -um - any, anyone
unus, -a, -un - one
urbs, urbis, f - a city, town
ut, conjunct. used with subjunctive - that, so that
uterque, utraque, utrumque, pron. and adj. - each (of two)
utinam, adv. - if only, would that
utrum, adv. introducing an indirect question - whether (an alternative is usually implied or expressed)
uxor, uxoris, f - a wife

V

vacuus, -a, -um - empty
vasto, vastare, -avi, -atum - to destroy, devastate
venia, -ae, f - pardon
venio, venire, vēni, ventum - to come; go
Venus, Veneris, f - Venus, the goddess of love and mother of Aeneas
ver, veris, n - the spring
vereor, vereri, veritus sum - to revere, respect, fear
veritas, veritatis, f - truth, the truth
verto, vertere, verti, versus - to turn
vesper, vesperi, m - the evening; the evening star
Vesta, -ae, f - Vesta, the goddess of the hearth; in her temple, her priestesses, the Vestal virgins, maintained a perpetual fire
via, -ae, f - a road, path, way
vicinus, -a, -um - near, neighboring
victor, victoris, m - conqueror, victor
video, videre, vidi, visum - to see, look at
vinco, vincere, vici, victum - to conquer, defeat
violentia, -ae, f - violence
vir, viri, m - a man; husband
vivo, vivere, vixi, victum - to be alive, live
voco, vocare, vocavi, vocatum - to call, summon
volo, velle, volui, ——— - to wish, will, want (no 4th principal part)
    irreg. pres. indicative - **volo, vis, vult, volumus, vultis, volunt**
    irreg. pres. subjunctive - **velim, velis, velit, velimus, velitis, velint**
vos, vobis - you (plu.)
vox, vocis, f - a voice
vultur, vulturis, m - a vulture, a bird of prey often used as an omen

English-Latin Glossary

A
about - de
advance - progredior, progredi, progressus est
Aeneas - Aeneas, -ae, m; acc. - Aenean
all - omnes, omnia (plural)
always - semper, adv.
ambassador - legatus, -i, m
ancient - antiquus, -a, -um
announce - nuntio, nuntiare, nuntiavi, nuntiatum + acc. of the announcement + dat. pers.
to be angry - irascor, irasci, iratus sum
Apollo - Apollo, Apollinis, m
aqueduct - aquaeductus, aquaeductūs, m
aquilifer - aquilifer, -feri, m (standard-bearer)
arrow - sagitta, -ae, f

B
bad - malus, -a, -um
battle - proelium, proelii, n
to be - sum, esse, fui, futurus
beg - oro, orare, oravi, oratum + acc. pers.
better - melior, melius
boldly - audacter
book - liber, libri, m
brave - fortis, forte
   bravely - fortiter
break - transitive - frango, frangere, fregi, fractum
intransitive - use passive voice (frangor)
bride - sponsa, -ae, f
bridge - pons, pontis, m
bring - adduco, adducere, adduxi, adductum
Britain - Britannia, -ae, f
Briton - Britannus, -i, m
build - aedifico, aedificare, aedificavi, aedificatum
but - sed

C
Caesar - Caesar, Caesaris, m
call - voco, vocare, vocavi, vocatum
camp (army) - castra, -orum, n. plu.
cat - feles, felis, f
Catiline - Catilina, a Roman aristocrat who tried to foment revolution against the Republic in 63 BC, when Cicero was consul. Cicero delivered four memorable orations against Catiline (two in the Senate and two to the Roman people) that were instrumental in foiling Catiline's plot.
choose - eligo, eligere, elegi, electum
citizen - civis, civis, m/f
city - urbs, urbis, f
civil - civilis, -e
cloud - nubes, nubis, f
collect - cogo, cogere, coegi, coactum
come - venio, venire, veni, ventum
command - impero, imperare, imperavi, imperatum + dat. pers.
commander - dux, ducis, m; imperator, -oris, m
commit (a crime) - perficio, perficere, perfeci, perfectum
conquer - vinco, vincere, vici, victum
consult - consulo, consulere, consului, consultum
country - terra, terrae, f
courage - virtus, virtutis, f
craftsman - faber, fabri, m
crime - scelus, sceleris, n
criticize - accuso, accusare, -avi, -atum
cross - transeo, transire, transivi, transitum
crowded - frequens, frequentis
Cupid - Cupido, Cupidinis, m

D
danger - periculum, -i, n
dangerous - periculosus, -a, -um
dark - obscurus, -a, -um
demand - postulo, postulare, postulavi, postulatum
depart from - exeo, exire, exii, exitum + ex + abl.
desire - cupio, cupere, cupivi, cupitum
desirous - cupidus, -a, -um
Dido - Dido, Didonis, f
do - facio, facere, feci, factum
distant - remotus, -a, -um
duct - ductus, ductus, m

E
easy - facilis, facile
   easily - faciliter
   more easily - facilius
empire - imperium, -i, n
encourage - hortor, hortari, hortatus sum
enemy - hostis, hostis, m/f (usually plural)
envoy - legatus, -i, m

escape from - fugio, fugere, fūgī, fugitum + abl.
everyone - omnis, omnis (each person); omnes, omnium (all people)
expand (transitive) - extendo, extendere, extendi, extentus

F

far - longe
father - pater, patris, m
fear, be afraid - metuo, metuere, metui; timeo, timere, timui, timitum; vereor, vereri, veritus sum
feel shame - verecundor, verecundari
fierce - ferox, ferocis
fight - pugno, pugnare, pugnavi, pugnatum
flee - fugio, fugere, fugi, fugitum
follow - sequor, sequi, secutus
food - cibus, cibi, m
forest - silva, silvae, f
foretell - praedico, praedicere, praedixi, praedictum
fortify - munio, munire, munivi, munitum
found (a city) - condo, condere, condidi, conditum
free - libero, liberare, liberavi, liberatum
frightening - horribilis, -e
from - ex + abl.

G

general - dux, ducis, m; imperator, -oris, m
girl - puella, -ae, f
go - proficiscor, proficisci, profectus sum; eo, ire, ii (ivi), itum
good - bonus, -a, -um
great - magnus, -a, -um

H

have - habeo, habere, habui, habitum
hear - audio, audire, audivi, auditum
Helvetii - Helvetii, Helvetiorum, m plu.
Hercules - Hercules, Herculis, m
his - eius; reflexive - suus, -a, um
history - historia, historiae, f
homeland - patria, -ae, f
hope - spes, spei, f
hurl - iacio, iacere, ieci, iactum

I

if - si
if only - utinam
ignore - ignore, ignorare, ignoravi, ignoratum
immortality - immortalitas, immortalitatis, f
into - in + acc.
interesting - iucundus, -a, -um
invade - invado, invadere, invasi, invasum

J

javelin - pilum, -i, n
jump down - desilio, desilire, desilui, desultum
jump over - transilio, transilire, transilui, ———
just - iustus, -a, -um

K

keep quiet - taceo, tacere, tacui, tacitum
kill - occido, occidere, occidi, occisum; neco, necare, necavi, necatum
king - rex, regis, m
know - cognosco, cognoscere, cognovi, cognitum

L

labor - labor, laboris, m
land - terra, terrae, f
land beyond the Po River - Transpadanus, -i, m
large - magnus, -a, -um
larger - maior, maius
Latinus - Latinus, -i, m
leave - relinquo, relinquere, relinqui, relictus
letter - epistula, -ae, f
life - vita, -ae, f
lion - leo, leonis, m
long - longus, -a, -um
too long, longest - longissimus, -a, -um
long time - diu
look for - quaero, quaerere, quaesivi, quaesitum
lose - perdo, perdere, perdidi, perditum

M

to make - facio, facere, feci, factum
maid - ancilla, -ae, f
man - homo, hominis, m; vir, viri, m
many - multi, -ae, -a
mind - mens, mentis, f
mother - mater, matris, f
mountain - mons, montis, m
my - meus, -a, -um

N

neighboring - vicinus, -a, -um
never - numquam
nevertheless - tamen
night - nox, noctis, f

O

omen - omen, ominis, n
on - in (prep.) + acc.
or - vel
oracle - oraculum, -i, n
oration - oratio, orationis, f

to give an oration - habere orationem
order - impero, imperare + dat. pers. and ut + subjunctive; iubeo, iubere, iussi, iussum + acc. + inf.
our - noster, -tra, -trum
outcome - eventum, -i, n

P

parent - parens, parentis, m
peace - pax, pacis, f
people - populus, populi, m
perform - facio, facere, feci, factum
place - locus, -i, m
plan - consilium, -i, n
pleasant - iucundus, -a, -um
   more pleasantly - iucundius
poem - carmen, carminis, n
Po River, land beyond the - Transpadanus, -i, m
prepare - paro, parare, paravi, paratum
pretty - bellus, -a, -um
promise - polliceor, polliceri, pollicitus sum
proud - superbus, -a, -um
punish - punio, punire, punivi, punitum

Q

keep quiet - taceo, tacere, tacui, tacitum

R

read - lego, legere, legi, lectum
repair - renovo, renovare, renovavi, renovatum
river - flumen, fluminis, n
Remus - Remus, -i, m
Roman (noun) - Romanus, Romani, m
Roman (adj.) - Romanus, -a, -um
Romulus - Romulus, -i, m
rough - asper, aspera, asperum

S

Sabine - Sabinus, -i, m
safe - tutus, -a, -um; incolumis, -e
sail - navigo, navigare, navigavi, navigatum
sailor - nauta, nautae, m
save - servo, servare, servavi, servatum
say - dico, dicere, dixi, dictum
sea - mare, maris, n
see - video, videre, vidi, visum
seek - peto, petere, petivi, petitum
Senate - Senatus, -ūs, m
send - mitto, mitere, misi, missum
feel shame - verecundor, verecundari, ———
sharp - acer, acris, acre
   sharper - acrior, acrius
shining - candidus, -a. -um

ship - navis, navis, f
shoot (an arrow) - iacio, iacere, ieci, iactum
keep silent - taceo, tacere, tacui, tacitum
sing - cano, canere, cecini, ———
sister - soror, sororis, f
slave - servus, -i, m
sleep - dormio, dormire, dormivi, dormitum
small - parvus, -a, -um
so - tam, tantum, adv.
soldier - miles, militis, m
so long - tamdiu, adv.
so many times - totiens
some - aliqui, aliqua, aliquod
son - filius, filii, m
sooner - citius, adv.
speak - dico, dicere, dixi, dictum
spend the winter - hiemo, hiemare, hiemavi, hiematurus
star - sidus, sideris, n
story - fabula, fabulae, f
strong - fortis, forte
sundial - horologium, -i, n
sweetly - suaviter

T

temple - templum, -i, n
terrain - locus, -i, m
terrible - horribilis, -e
that - ut
think - puto, putare, putavi, putatum
this - hic, haec, hoc
through - per, prep. + acc.
throw - iacio, iacere, ieci, iactum
time - tempus, temporis, n
tragic - tragicus, -a, -um
treaty - foedus, foederis, n
Turnus - Turnus, -i, m
twelve - duodecim (indeclinable)

U

use - utor, uti, usus sum + abl.

V

Venus - Venus, Veneris, f
voice - vox, vocis, f

W

wall - murus, -i, m
wander - vagor, vagari, vagitus sum
want - volo, velle, volui (irreg.)
wage (war) - gero, gerere, gessi, gestum
war - bellum, -i, n

English-Latin Glossary

water - aqua, aquae, f
weapon - telum, n
weep - fleo, flere, flevi, fletum
well - bene
whether - utrum
    whether . . . or - utrum . . . an
where - ubi
white - albus, -a, -um
who, which - qui, quae, quod
wild - ferox, ferocis
winter, to spend the - hiemo, hiemare, hiemavi, hiematurus

wolf - lupus, lupi, m
wonder – miror, mirari, miratus sum
work (verb) - laboro, laborare, laboravi, laboratum
work (noun) - opus, operis, n
write - scribo, scribere, scripsi, scriptum

Y

you - singular - tu, tui, tibi, te, te; plural - vos, vestrum/vestri, vobis, vos, vobis

Chapter Index of "Lingua Latina Ubique" Entries

A
ad hoc   Chapter 7
ad hominem   Chapter 5
ad nauseam   Chapter 10
agenda   Chapter 6
alibi   Chapter 11
alma mater   Chapter 10
Altima   Chapter 12

B
bona fides   Chapter 14
bona fide   Chapter 14

C
carpe diem   Chapter 1
casus belli   Chapter 3
caveat emptor   Chapter 8
cf. (confer)   Chapter 9
citius, altius, fortius   Chapter 15

D
data   Chapter 10
de facto   Chapter 5

E
e pluribus unum   Chapter 1
e.g. (exempli gratia)   Chapter 13
et al. (et alii)   Chapter 9
etc. (et cetera)   Chapter 8
excelsior   Chapter 3

F
Formica   Chapter 12

H
habeas corpus   Chapter 11

I
ibidem (ibid.)   Chapter 9
idem (id.)   Chapter 9
i.e. (id est)   Chapter 9
imprimatur   Chapter 8
ipso facto   Chapter 13

L
loc. cit. (loco citato)   Chapter 9

M
magna cum laude   Chapter 1
magnum opus   Chapter 1
media   Chapter 10
memoranda   Chapter 6
modus operandi   Chapter 8
modus vivendi   Chapter 6
mutatis mutandis   Chapter 4

N
ne plus ultra   Chapter 15
non sequitur   Chapter 2

O
op. cit. (opere citato)   Chapter 9
Optima   Chapter 12

P
Pergo   Chapter 12
per se   Chapter 5
persona non grata   Chapter 14
placebo   Chapter 2
post hoc ergo propter hoc   Chapter 15
prima facie   Chapter 14
Prius   Chapter 12
propaganda   Chapter 6

Q
quid pro quo   Chapter 13
quorum   Chapter 2

R
referendum   Chapter 7

S
Semper Fidelis   Chapter 5
sine qua non   Chapter 2
status quo   Chapter 4
subpoena   Chapter 11
sui generis   Chapter 7

Chapter Index of "Lingua Latina Ubique" Entries

V

verbatim   Chapter 4
Vespa   Chapter 12
veto   Chapter 14

vice versa   Chapter 7
Volvo   Chapter 12
vox populi   Chapter 3

www.ingramcontent.com/pod-product-compliance
Lightning Source LLC
Chambersburg PA
CBHW081218230426
43666CB00015B/2779